Advance Praise for *Children Come First*:

"Dr. Irving has provided a practical, thoughtfully researched book for parents who are contemplating or going through divorce. It offers an opportunity for parents and their children to go through the transitional phase of divorce in the least destructive way."

— **Faye Mishna**, Ph.D., R.S.W.,
Professor and Dean, Factor-Inwentash
Faculty of Social Work, University of Toronto

"This valuable book provides parents, lawyers, judges, mediators, and children with useful resources and Dr. Irving's inimitable wisdom. He has helped thousands of families to put their children first. Anyone who is contemplating a separation, is involved in a custody dispute, or is parenting children post-separation should read this book."

— **Martha McCarthy**, family lawyer,
Martha McCarthy & Company

"Dr. Irving has created an easy-to-read guide for parents going through family breakup, from helping them to appreciate the dynamics and emotions they are experiencing to providing actual examples of parenting plans and schedules. In my own twenty-five years as a family mediator, I often wished that such a book was available for my clients. I give it my wholehearted recommendation."

— **Janet Seitlin**, Esq.,
Adjunct Professor,
University of Miami Law School

CHILDREN COME FIRST

Mediation, Not Litigation When Marriage Ends

Howard H. Irving, Ph.D.

DUNDURN PRESS

TORONTO

Copyright © Howard H. Irving, 2011

All rights reserved. No part of this publication may be reproduced, stored in a retrieval system, or transmitted in any form or by any means, electronic, mechanical, photocopying, recording, or otherwise (except for brief passages for purposes of review) without the prior permission of Dundurn Press. Permission to photocopy should be requested from Access Copyright.

Project Editor: Michael Carroll
Editor: Allison Hirst
Design: Jennifer Scott
Printer: Marquis

Library and Archives Canada Cataloguing in Publication

Irving, Howard H., 1936-
    Children come first : mediation, not litigation when marriage ends / by Howard H. Irving.

Includes bibliographical references and index.
Issued also in electronic format.
ISBN 978-1-55488-795-8

1. Divorce mediation. 2. Custody of children. I. Title.

HQ814.I783 2011   306.89   C2010-902691-8

1 2 3 4 5   15   14   13   12   11

 Conseil des Arts du Canada   Canada Council for the Arts   ONTARIO ARTS COUNCIL CONSEIL DES ARTS DE L'ONTARIO

We acknowledge the support of the **Canada Council for the Arts** and the **Ontario Arts Council** for our publishing program. We also acknowledge the financial support of the **Government of Canada** through the **Canada Book Fund** and **Livres Canada Books**, and the **Government of Ontario** through the **Ontario Book Publishers Tax Credit** program, and the **Ontario Media Development Corporation**.

Care has been taken to trace the ownership of copyright material used in this book. The author and the publisher welcome any information enabling them to rectify any references or credits in subsequent editions.

J. Kirk Howard, President

Printed and bound in Canada.
www.dundurn.com

Dundurn Press	Gazelle Book Services Limited	Dundurn Press
3 Church Street, Suite 500	White Cross Mills	2250 Military Road
Toronto, Ontario, Canada	High Town, Lancaster, England	Tonawanda, NY
M5E 1M2	LA1 4XS	U.S.A. 14150

In memory of my parents, Samuel and Sylvia Irving, and of my late colleague, Dr. Michael Benjamin

Contents

Acknowledgements

The inspiration for this book came from my own personal experience with divorce mediation gained from my family mediation practice and from my teaching and research over many years. To the many families who shared with me their hurt and courage, I am truly grateful. They have taught me so much.

A great deal is owed to my professional colleagues who worked with me at the University of Toronto, Family Mediation Program. To name only a few: Merrill Barber, Guil Arbour, Jennifer Shuber, Virginia Hammara, Heather Swartz, Andrea Litvak, Melanie Kraft, and Ka Tat Tsang.

I am truly grateful to the leaders and writers in the mediation field who have influenced me and helped develop the ideas in this book — Isolina Ricci, Joan Kelly, Donald Saposnek, Hugh McIssac, Judith Wallerstein, Mary Duryee, Edward Kruk, Philip Epstein, Judith Ryan, Barbara Landau, and Judge Harvey Brownstone.

Through numerous drafts and edits, invaluable discussions with my associate Merrill Barber and my daughter Jennifer Irving Kochman helped me immeasurably to gain a better perspective and to make this book a reality. I am truly indebted to them.

During the early phases of the development of this book, I received valuable assistance from Don Bastian and Guil Arbour. I also want to thank Michael Carroll and the staff at Dundurn Press for their expert assistance. I am especially grateful to Allison Hirst for her thoughtful advice and invaluable editing of the manuscript.

On a more personal note, I am deeply appreciative for the patience and understanding from my wife, Fahla, and my children, Jonathan, Jennifer, Adam, and Jay, who above all taught me the real value of divorce mediation. I only hope that I continue to be a good student.

Introduction

When a marriage is over, it is not a time for retribution and revenge, but rather the time to make a positive adjustment while providing for and protecting the children.

For three decades I have championed the use of divorce mediation as an alternative to the adversary court system in order to save couples and their children from the bitter legacy of legal wrangling and winner-take-all custody battles. I have mediated more than two thousand cases during that time. If I have learned anything, it is this: if the adversary system takes a bad situation and makes it worse, divorce mediation can take the same situation and make it "less bad" — and often better.

My previous books were academic in approach because divorce mediation was new to family law and the theory behind it needed to be established. In addition, as a university professor, my writing was evidence-based, set up to be reviewed and discussed by other scholars and members of the legal fraternity for accuracy.

With this book, however, I am taking advantage of my research and experience to speak directly to parents who are going through a divorce. While the book is of value to anyone involved in any way with divorce — including marriage counsellors, family mediators, and lawyers — it is written primarily to help couples themselves, especially those with children.

In this book, I will do my best to

- enlighten couples about the nature of the adversary system and the dangers it poses for their children and for themselves.
- describe the benefits of divorce mediation, taking readers through the mediation process.
- give helpful pointers to children to help them through their parents' divorce.
- give advice to parents, to help them protect their children from the effects of divorce.
- take parents through the process of building a shared-parenting plan that puts the children's interests uppermost, while taking their own unique situations into account.

I have illustrated *Children Come First* with many examples from my mediation practice (though with names and identities changed, to protect my clients' privacy).

The book's audience is large. It includes

- men and women considering or going through a divorce. Fifty percent of couples married today will divorce, as will a significant number of couples in a subsequent marriage.
- couples considering divorce mediation as an alternative to the adversary system, or already in the divorce mediation process.
- concerned family and friends of those going through a divorce, including grandparents who wish to maintain contact with their grandchildren.

- people looking for a less expensive approach to divorce given the financially turbulent times.
- lawyers who are themselves concerned about the adversary system and would like their clients to consider a better way to proceed.
- mediators, who may give it to those considering, or going through, mediation.

The chapters move simply and logically from the dangers of the adversarial approach and advantages of divorce mediation to shared-parenting plans, including how you can create one that is best for your children and your own situation.

Divorce mediation offers you an alternative to the traditional adversary approach to divorce. However, it is important to note that mediation is not magic. It is not a single brilliant intervention that changes the face of the family and sets everything right. Rather, it is a thoughtful approach to the dynamics underlying family systems and conflict. It can involve the creative use of a wide variety of interventions, custom-made to suit particular situations. When these are effective, the results can be truly dramatic. More often, successful outcomes result from simple hard work by the parents as the mediator keeps them focused on the children, blocks unproductive conduct, suggests options and alternatives, clarifies the consequences of a failure to agree, and uses the parents' love for their children as the lever for agreement.

My hope is that this book will protect you and your family from needless suffering and harm for many years to come, and will put into play an opportunity for positive parenting — a rainbow after the rain, so to speak.

1

What Is
Divorce Mediation?

*Divorce mediation is a voluntary process with
an impartial third party (a family mediator)
who helps families identify and clarify issues
together, assisting them in coming to an agreement on some or all of these issues.*

You and your partner may have agreed that divorce is the only
recourse to your deteriorating relationship. Or only one of
you may feel that way. Yet both of you are concerned about
the welfare of your children.

ADVERSARIAL DIVORCE

If you are like most couples, you think your only path is to
seek the advice of lawyers and begin the messy process of
dividing assets, property ... and children.

Yes, once you have started down this road, your children
will be in danger of becoming treated as another asset, along
with cars, the family house, the cottage, and any retirement
saving plans that may have been started. The winner-takes-
all approach to traditional divorce proceedings takes the hurt,
pride, and genuine disappointment of the parents and loads

it onto the next generation. It is all too well known how damaging divorce can be for children ... and their own marriages down the road.

Ironically, lawyers and judges themselves are increasingly disenchanted with the current adversary method of resolving family disputes. This method is based on an addiction to winning. Lawyers acknowledge that the adversary system takes care of the mechanical separation and legal technicalities of divorce but that it does little to help parents and their children with the emotional trauma they are going through. As Justice Donald B. King of California puts it:

> The adversary system is a monster with a life and a momentum of its own that too often places the case beyond the control of the parties, their attorneys, and the judges. The system creates an accusatory atmosphere that destroys communication and co-operation. The adversary system works well for litigants who will never see each other again, but it is too slow, too expensive, too impersonal, and does not help divorcing spouses who will have to remain in contact with each other for years because of children or support obligations.[1]

As you may already be finding out yourself, the legal system often thrives on protracted litigation. This litigation inevitably ends up alienating both parents and children. Lawyers, trained to zealously advocate for the rights and benefits of their adult clients, rarely have expertise in family dynamics or child development. Family dynamics are not considered legitimate legal problems. The adversary system in general, and the area of family law specifically, lands families in a process that's not set up to bring about humane resolutions.

Divorce mediation, in contrast, does what traditional law cannot: it promotes parental co-operation and goodwill, encouraging parents to accept mutual responsibility for their children by creating detailed parenting plans that are in the children's best interests.

Divorce mediation will help *you* and the legal system to treat your children not as assets to be divided but as innocents who must be protected, in every way possible, from the fallout of your breakup.

THE DEFINITION OF DIVORCE MEDIATION

Some years ago, I was intrigued when I heard a speaker at a university conference on divorce mediation say that he was going to define exactly what a mediator does. Here's what he said:

> One day I was sitting in the kitchen having breakfast with my kids. I looked out the window and saw that the week's garbage hadn't been taken out. I asked my son, since it was his turn that week, why he hadn't done so. He pointed to my daughter and said, "No, it's her turn because she said if I gave her a ride to the party, she'd do my week." I thought to myself, "Now I have to mediate this." And this is what I did: I took the garbage out. And that, ladies and gentlemen, is what mediators do. They take out the garbage.

Divorce mediation does indeed include taking out the garbage, but it is much more than that. Following is a fuller description.

Divorce mediation is a voluntary process with an impartial third party (a family mediator) who helps families identify and clarify issues between them, assisting them in coming to an agreement on some or all of these issues. The goal of successful divorce mediation is to help family members arrive at an agreement that is in the best interest of the family. It is very important for the family to maintain control and be involved in these decisions. The premise of mediation is that the parents are partners in decision-making regarding their children in the weeks, months, and years following the divorce.

Divorce mediation does not deal with fault, find blame, give legal advice, or make decisions for others. In fact, ideally it begins by exploring the possibility that the couple can be reconciled. Sometimes mediators recommend a marriage counsellor for a couple and are happy never to see them again because they know they have made a fresh start on their marriage.

Mediation fosters a sense of individual empowerment, as well as the ability to respond co-operatively to changed circumstances. The consensual nature of mediation can, for example, lessen the probability of child support violations and bitter custody disputes.

Within the adversarial framework, the angry spouse often projects his or her anger and resentment onto the divorce action itself. The spouse's resistance to amicable settlement is expressed in adversarial language, such as, "Fine, divorce me. But I'm not going to lose the car, the house, the children." In litigation-based divorce, personal bitterness, for whatever reason, is joined to the legal system's compulsion to win. The litigant sees the spouse as an opponent who must be defeated, taking the attitude of a sports team that the best defence is a strong offence.

Mediation gives you and your spouse an exit ramp from this all-or-nothing thinking. It is important to note that you and your spouse, should you go through the mediation process, will each need to retain legal counsel for the purpose of making sure your agreement is fair and what you wanted. However, the mediation process will keep your lawyers informed of progress and final decisions, instead of having them manage the process competitively. Many lawyers, however, are supportive of mediation and will join what becomes the mediation — legal teams helping families resolve their issues constructively. A story from my own experience may serve as a helpful illustration of how a good mediator will approach helping you and your children.

My wife and I had just bought and installed bunk beds for our twin sons Adam and Jay. "You're a mediator," my wife said. "How are you going to work with the boys to determine which one gets the top bunk?"

"Well, I could suggest that one of them takes the bottom bunk for the first week, and the other the top bunk, and then they could switch...."

"For goodness sake, this isn't a custody issue," she said. "There ought to be an easier way."

"Okay, maybe I'll flip a coin," I said.

When the boys came home, we showed them the new beds. "Great, I'll take the top," one of them said.

"And I'll take the bottom," said the other.

This is a great example of how important self-determination is in the mediation process. As a mediator, I strive to empower people to make their *own* decisions and their *own* parenting plans based on self-determination. You know what's best. Get your mediator to help you implement it.

Ideally, divorce mediation paves the way for each parent to agree on what they will do to safeguard their children so the whole family can make a new beginning.

"Divorce mediation" is the main term I will use in this book. You may come across related terms, such as:

- *Therapeutic family mediation.* A phrase I coined to cover the whole process of working with couples and their children both outside and within a legal context. In Therapeutic Mediation, emotions are dealt with to get at the subtext of the issues in a rational way.

- *Family mediation.* A legal term used to describe mediation within the area of family law.
- *Collaborative law.* A term used to describe legal processes in which the parties and lawyers involved are committed to turning down the adversarial volume in disputes and agree that they will not litigate.
- *Alternative dispute resolution (ADR).* A grab-bag term to cover methods increasingly used by court systems in various jurisdictions. These methods try to head disputes off at the pass before they can get caught up in the adversary approach. Some court systems even require that a case be given the chance for ADR treatment before it can go through the regular system.
- *Arbitration.* Far more structured than mediation, it's where the arbitrator really acts as a judge and makes an award which can be nonbinding or binding.

All of these terms and approaches are part of a growing trend to help parties settle their disputes in a more humane, rational, and time-effective and cost-effective way.

THE BENEFITS OF DIVORCE MEDIATION

There are two main benefits of divorce mediation. The first is that it protects children from the plague of parental squabbles over custody. Couples who go through divorce mediation are usually fuelled by the attitude and commitment that the kids come first. These parents make sure that the division of assets, the creation of the parenting schedule, and the hard work of transforming the marriage and family relationship are based on what is best for their kids. They take responsibility for their own situations and want to avoid passing their own disappointment down to their children through the adversary system.

The second main benefit of divorce mediation is that it extends this protection of the kids beyond the divorce and into the years that follow the initial breakup of the parents. It does this by helping parents to negotiate shared-parenting plans. This book shows that shared parenting is superior to what comes out of traditional adversarial outcomes. Some children never fully recover from the latter experience. Like mediation itself, shared parenting is based on the assumption that the parents wish to work together for the sake of their children. The following benefits have been substantiated through evidence-based mediation completed by researchers during the past several years.

Other benefits of divorce mediation are that it:

- creates a fair and co-operative process for divorcing/divorced couples in conflict;
- sets out and clarifies the issues in dispute between them;
- gives them an opportunity to consider reconciliation;
- encourages parents to put the best interests of their children ahead of their own interests; and
- arrives at a settlement on the issues that is mutually acceptable and that is both fair and equitable in light of the circumstances.

There is virtual consensus across a range of studies that more than 70 percent of all cases seen in family mediation end in full or partial agreement. Further research identifies family mediation as an effective approach based on a range of other outcomes, including client satisfaction, perceived fairness, client sense of empowerment, financial support, parent-child relations, and parental co-operation.[2]

CHILDREN COME FIRST

SHARED PARENTING

Shared parenting is in fact the other main concept dealt with in this book. If divorce mediation is a more humane way to divorce, shared parenting is a more humane way to deal with custody issues. Think about that word "custody." One of its definitions is "incarceration." In a sense, the aim of custody battles is to decide who gets to incarcerate the kids! That is fundamentally different from a process that seeks to involve both parents in caring for their kids. Custody implies ownership and none of us should think or act as if we "own" our children.

So, to put it in a nutshell, this book guides you to and through the divorce mediation process so you can develop a mature, reasonable shared-parenting plan that gives your children what they want most: the love and care of both of their parents.

Children in a shared-parenting arrangement benefit from having more time — and a more authentic kind of relationship — with each parent. It should be noted that shared parenting is not joint custody, the arrangement in which the kids spend half of the time with each parent. It could take on that shape in some situations. But the most important thing about shared parenting is that no matter what the schedule is for the children, each parent is considered equal when it comes to taking responsibility and making major decisions for the children.

In this approach the children's lives aren't interrupted when they have to visit the other parent. As Everett has said, "visits are for hospitals and funeral parlours, not for seeing your own children."[3] Shared parenting builds a new kind of family structure around the children of divorce, giving them the best possible chance to get what they need as they mature.

THE EFFECTS OF PARENTAL BEHAVIOUR
ON CHILDREN

Study after study tells us with certainty that children adjust better to family separation, suffering fewer negative effects, when their parents minimize conflict and show themselves to be emotionally mature.

Knowing this, society must not offer as a first resort for separating families an adversary system that by its very nature often heightens conflict and threatens emotional well-being. Experience and academic research tell us, for example, that the language of affidavits — a primary tool of custody litigation — can actually encourage parents to depersonalize each other and cast each other in the role of the enemy. Legal procedures can be used to lay blame and cause lasting hurt. By using mediation, in contrast, parents can build a shared understanding of a parenting problem and a co-operative attempt at resolution.

Parents are learning to distinguish their own problems from their responsibility to their children. They are learning that it's not fair to pull their kids into their own conflict. Children of divorce react in a variety of ways, but often those ways reflect the actions of the parents. Like a mirror, the various emotional phases of divorce may be seen in the actions of the children. You must be able to see that your children deserve fair and decent treatment no matter how problematic your own relationship may be.

Hugh McIsaac, a prominent family mediator, illustrates another key point in favour of divorce mediation. He says of his work as a mediator:

> We were able to help the parties reach their own solution and separate the parental issues from the spousal ones. We recognized the need to focus on underlying

issues and needs — to focus on *what* was wrong, not *who* was wrong.

The idea was that divorce was a reorganization of the family, not an end of the family, and thus the concept of not being divorced *from* someone but being divorced *to* them was being conceived. "Separating together" became the new catch phrase for divorcing couples who were putting their children first.[4]

THE EVOLUTION OF DIVORCE MEDIATION

Let me close this chapter with a few reflections on how this "better way" of dealing with divorce has evolved.

Mediation has been around for centuries. It is among the oldest practices of community life. The Beth Din, a Jewish religious court that began thousands of years ago, is one example in Jewish culture.

Arbitration and mediation is a long-time part of Japanese culture, too. Japan has a population of 127 million people served by 23,119 lawyers. The United States has a population of 307 million served by 1.14 million lawyers. Without question, the United States and Canada make up the most litigation-prone area in the world. Why the difference? The difference is because the two systems rest on very different premises. While the North American legal process is aimed at reaching "justice," the Japanese process is aimed at restoring harmony.

The Japanese legal system sets out from the very beginning to harmonize the views of the antagonists. Since the restoration of harmony is the main theme of its concept of justice, the avoidance of litigation is a high priority. Most disputes in that country are settled by using mediation techniques rather than by going to trial.

China serves as another example of a country that prefers mediation over litigation. For the past several years I have been consulting on and teaching family mediation in that country. The experience has taught me the value of putting families ahead of individual rights, as opposed to the opposite practice in North America. Chinese families highly value the notion of saving face. They often cite the proverb "Going to law is losing a cow for the sake of a cat."

During my many visits to Hong Kong and mainland China over the past few years, I have had the opportunity to work with a number of Chinese families and Chinese mediators. This culminated in my writing two books that were translated into Chinese dealing with mediating with Chinese families. There is no question that the Chinese are looking to empower families who are going through separation by using the mutuality approach rather than the adversary one.

Mediation programs in North America are partly the result of the frustration of family court judges with the premise and approach of the legal system. As they look at divorcing couples standing before the bench with their prepared cases and their lawyers, they know full well that mere decisions on custody, access, and maintenance will not really help them. Subsequently, many of these judges have been happy to see the development of mediation programs to help couples cope with their more important challenge: protecting their children.

Although mediation in North America is growing in use and becoming better known to the public, it is still very much in its infancy. For example, a senior family court judge introduced me before I addressed an audience of approximately eighty judges with the words: "And now Dr. Howard Irving will speak about *meditation*."

I was caught off-guard by the obvious gaffe, but on looking out at my audience, I realized that no one had actually taken note. So I took this as a good sign and proceeded. And ever since then I have maintained that it is a good thing that some mediators have suggested that their clients actually meditate to help them cope with a stressful situation. A recent newspaper article said of me, "This Guru would rather mediate than meditate."

2

Why Divorce Mediation Is the Better Way

Victory creates hatred. Defeat creates suffering. Those who are wise strive for neither victory nor defeat.
— Buddha

A major goal of divorce mediation is to help couples like you to act rationally and responsibly in order to make compromises that benefit your children. I realize that acting responsibly in this way is often not easy for couples caught up in the drama of separation and divorce.

Divorce could be said to be a "perfect storm," in which all the "right" conditions for creating maximum marital and family suffering come together. These conditions include the couple's hurt, or perhaps even shock, that their marriage is coming apart. This in most cases sparks strong feelings of anger, resentment, and regret. The fact that society accepts divorce as a solution to personal problems, rather than seeing it more accurately as a different and much worse problem, is also a factor. Finally, all of the above conditions are channelled into a legal system that feeds on parents' fears that if they don't fight for their rights they could lose everything, including their children. Throughout the process, children are left at the mercy of lightning strikes, torrents of rain, and high-velocity winds.

The following is a letter that I wrote to one couple who were stuck in the perfect storm:

Dear Barbara and Charles,

I find myself caught in the middle between two parents who have lost trust and respect for each other. This has resulted in an inability for each of you to move forward in a shared-parenting relationship.

I have tried to focus in our mediation on your children's rights and needs, and not on parental rights or taking sides. I have tried to have you set aside your unresolved marital issues for the sake of the children.

Unfortunately, the mediation is being compromised by the anger, hurt and resentment of how the marriage ended. This is now compounded by the inability for each of you to reach a cooperative parenting plan. It appears that both of you are on opposite ends of your respective parental positions. Clearly the threat of litigation has exacerbated the situation, resulting in both families including extended family, being fearful and now having a lack of trust. This lack of trust has lead to a great deal of conflict, and in effect you're in the perfect storm. The unresolved marital issues and the unresolved parental issues have made things very difficult for us to benefit from the mediation process.

I find this both sad and ironic because each of you love your children and want to protect them more than anything from any fallout resulting in a conflictual separation.

I want to help both of you and especially the children get through this situation with little difficulty.

I'm confident that once the marital issues have been resolved, you will both move forward and be able to provide a more effective parenting plan for your children.

I have a great deal of empathy for both of you, and of course the children. I will continue to do my best to help you resolve some of the issues that you are dealing with and to create a much better relationship between both of you, knowing that the children will benefit from this.

Best regards,
Howard

If you are reading this book, I assume that you are heading toward or are already involved in divorce proceedings. Hopefully you have tried marital counselling as a first step. I know that this is an emotional time, but please give this chapter a chance to convince you that not only can you avoid the perfect storm of divorce but you can protect your children from it, too. I want to persuade you that the adversary approach to divorce is to be avoided at all costs. I want to show you why divorce mediation is the better way to go.

The rest of this chapter will examine the culture of divorce, the stress of divorce, and then some actual cases of divorce that took the traditional route.

BREAKING UP IS HARD TO DO

The odds makers will give you odds on almost everything: who will win the next election, what football team will make the Super Bowl, whether or not a certain stock will rise or fall. Odds are calculated on statistical probability and, if you are married, the probability of your being one of the two principal parties in a divorce action is one in two. If you are simply living and breathing in North America, the odds of your being involved with someone who is getting a divorce are better than even.

Just about everyone has had, or will have, the experience of standing by while relatives or close friends go through the painful process of divorce. Perhaps you have just met an old friend on the street and invited him or her to dinner. Casually, you include the marital partner in the invitation. There is an awkward silence, followed by their confession that they are separated, getting a divorce, or no longer in contact. In all probability this will lead to your hearing one side of the story. You are duly confused because both of these people are your friends. You stumble for the right words and inwardly you choose whether or not to become involved.

This is the casual experience with divorce — but many people will experience it more intimately.

This year alone, in North America over one million marriages will end. Three quarters of these will involve children. All will affect "satellite" figures: grandparents, brothers and sisters, friends. Divorce directly influences a whole system of people in addition to the principal parties. Clearly, we are facing a problem that has reached epidemic proportions. Recently, a stand-up comic remarked, "I've never been married but I tell people I'm divorced so they won't think something is wrong with me." Conservatively, ten million people will be closely tied to the one million divorces. The nuclear family (mother, father, and children) appears to be more extended than we usually acknowledge, and people who sometimes seem uninvolved when all is well become quite involved when things go wrong. And it's a sure thing that this problem is not going to get any better — at least not any time soon.

Although it is fashionable to discuss "the death of the family," the family remains the basic unit of our society. The family is still the primary source of psychological security and personality development. In fact, the whole point of this book is that divorce does not have to mean the "death" of your family. Through divorce mediation and shared parenting, as described in this book, you can stay on civil terms with your former spouse as both of you work together and on your own to ensure the safety and health of your children.

One thing is for sure: divorce through the adversary system is not the way to go. Divorce litigation is unique among legal actions because it is invariably accompanied by intense and intimate emotions. Divorce is rarely a clean piece of business with a clear-cut beginning and end; seldom can it be handled and simply filed away. When the psychological factors that affect the situation are not dealt with during the divorce process, the resulting complications plague the parties, often for the rest of their lives. There may be bitter acrimony over child custody and visitation rights. There may be continued court actions over non-payment of alimony and child support.

Over time the wounds of your divorce will heal. More often than not, however, you must go on seeing each other because there are children involved, and the wounds caused by the divorce action are constantly reopened.

What causes the wounds to be so deep? Recently, one of my clients told me that she was suffering the "death of a thousand cuts" because of the protracted litigation with her former husband. Why is a divorce one of the most serious of life's crises?

The answers to these two questions lie not only in the relationship of the couple but also in our legal system. A divorce action finds blame. It rewards one of the parties and punishes the other. This is complicated by the fact that usually one of the parties desires the divorce more strongly than the other.

It seems paradoxical to hope that the couple in the midst of finding blame nevertheless work constructively to compromise over their differences and minimize damage to their children. The psychological impact of the adversary system results in pitting the marital couple against each other, in what feels like mortal combat. It is a system that requires winners and losers. I saw an ad by a law firm at a bus stop that read: FAMILY LAW: 27 YEARS OF WINNING CASES. The difficulty with this ad is that one has a vision of twenty-seven years of the other side losing cases rather than a vision of a win-win result. One of the parties is demeaned and made to feel guilty. This situation naturally encouraged counterattacks. Given the emotional trauma that already exists in most cases, constructive communication between the spouses becomes even more difficult. In other words, people who are already at emotional risk and in need of support find themselves involved in a system which offers them no support and greatly increases the traumatic effects of the situation. They are caught in a downward emotional spiral.

THE STRESS OF DIVORCE

Divorce is not only prevalent in our culture, it also creates untold suffering and stress, stress similar to that experienced during the stages of grief that follow a death of a loved one. These are often referred to as "the seasons of stress" — predictable, stressful phases that divorced people experience as part of the continuing process of change. Stress affects the individual all along the road to divorce and after it: the outcome of changing relationships, old and new, often depends on the individual's ability to deal with stress at the time and also to prepare for or avert the next phase of stress. For divorcing parents like yourselves, it is the time for meeting the challenges of divorce transitions by being resilient and strong for both yourself and your children.

Seasons of Stress

• The stress of unresolved marital discord that leads to divorce.

• The stress of the divorce process itself.

• The stress of the immediate post-divorce period.

• The stress of constructing a new life with new relationships.

To generalize, it can be said that these stages comprise a continuum of potential stress, with stress at the beginning of the process, rising to a crescendo during and immediately after the divorce, and then subsiding again as your new life eventually emerges.[5]

The deterioration of a relationship causes anxiety as one tries again and again to patch up the problems and start over and to keep control over their own destiny. With each failure, they experience the slipping away of a life on which they have based all their hopes and into which they have poured all their energies.

At one end of the spectrum of troubled marriages are those that can be, and are, saved — the bond between spouses often stronger once the broken pieces are healed. Divorce is not inevitable in a problem marriage. At the other end of the spectrum are marriages that dissolve quietly and easily. Between these two extremes is the vast number of marriages that dissolve in a swirl of family problems.

Looking at the full range of divorce situations, there are some cases where it would be better for the kids if the parents stayed together. There are other situations where the kids would be better off if their parents divorced. A high-conflict intact marriage is sometimes more damaging to children than a divorce.

If you are involved in separation or divorce, you may be so emotionally distraught that you think the adversary approach is the only way to go. I hope the following will help you rethink your position.

THE CHALLENGES OF THE
ADVERSARIAL DIVORCE PROCESS

The effects of our legal system complicate and increase stress during the four seasons of stress described above.

Let's begin with the divorce process itself. A major cause of pain in most divorces is the fact that both parties are seldom at the same level of readiness to terminate the marriage. One inevitably consults a lawyer first. Most commonly, one of the partners has left or is about to leave. The other party feels rejected and abandoned. The rejected spouse who is unable to accept the fact that his or her partner will really go through with the divorce is frequently willing to agree to almost anything in the vain hope that this will bring the spouse back.

In the majority of cases, the divorce is initiated by one spouse against the will of the other. The rejected spouse often engages in a reuniting strategy. This parent carefully avoids all conflict, bowing to the other parent's "superior knowledge and insight." Of course, the underlying hope is that this compliant attitude will cause the other parent to realize that divorcing is a mistake, and the two can be reunited.

The following example illustrates the conflicting emotions of one couple I worked with in mediation.

When Alice Brown contacted me, she was desperate. She began by trying to impress me with what a wonderful person her estranged husband was. At the same time, she was giving me the facts about how he plotted and planned his leaving. He had transferred all his assets into a corporate name. He also had several meetings with his lawyers and purchased a home in the name of his new girlfriend. Alice's trauma was intensified because she found out about all of this from her son, not her spouse.

Alice was too emotional about her situation to function rationally. She felt prepared to accept little or no maintenance in order not to jeopardize the chances for reconciliation. "I'm not concerned about the money," she said, "I just want him back. You can't imagine how lonely I've been the past seven weeks."

The rejected party is often so upset by the realization that the spouse is actually leaving they cannot sort out what the real financial needs may be. And more importantly, they cannot properly understand the children's needs. Sometimes depression is so great that an inadequate financial arrangement is accepted simply to get the whole procedure over and done with. Conversely, the guilt of the party who is leaving may be so great that an unreasonably high amount of maintenance is offered. Time passes and eventually resentment rises to the surface and results in further litigation.

The phrase "I didn't want this divorce" often implies "I didn't cause this divorce" or "I am not to blame." Revenge surfaces easily and proves the cliché that love and hate are two closely related emotions. This is the adversary system's cup of tea. It knows just what to do when a desire for revenge is in the air. The alleged guilty party is threatened with legal punishment.

John Wilson was angry and resentful because his wife had left him. Worse yet, her new male companion had been a mutual friend. He was so infuriated that his main concern was to hurt his wife in the deepest way possible. He kept repeating over and over again, whether to his lawyer or family or friends, that his wife was unfaithful, an unfit mother, and that there was no way in which she would ever get their children.

It is typical for the spurned spouse to adopt the view that he or she has been made to suffer all sorts of indignities. The result is to seek revenge in the form of money, or much worse, by using the children as a means of punishing the spouse or "getting even."

DON'T DIVORCE YOUR CHILDREN

What about your children? What are they in for if you take the adversary approach?

The children of divorce are taken on the ride of their lives. An earlier generation of moviegoers were given a close look at this phenomenon in the 1979 film *Kramer vs. Kramer*, starring Dustin Hoffman and Meryl Streep. In the movie, young Billy is taken care of by his workaholic father, who, through trial and error, turns his focus from work to his son and becomes a nurturing father. However, though she is the main cause of the divorce, Billy's mother wins the custody battle and Billy is wrested from his father.

Today, the trauma may be seen in the comic yet sad movie *The Squid and the Whale*, starring Jeff Daniels and Laura Linney. Set in Brooklyn in the 1980s, this movie shows the devastating effect of a couple's messy divorce on two sons: a sixteen-year-old who passes off a Pink Floyd song as his own in a talent show, and a twelve-year-old who descends into alcoholism. This film illustrates how it is the management of divorce, not the divorce itself, which harms kids most.

Disagreements between couples residing together under one roof are a direct example of conflict caused by such management. In fact, Martha McCarthy, who is an experienced family lawyer, admits that she has to go against her instincts when she tells her clients to stay in the family home no matter how bad the situation may be. She knows that the other side would use such an exit as a negative precedent in any subsequent custody deliberations.

"I hate giving that advice," she says. "Every time I give it, I hate hearing myself say it. I think it's awful."[6] McCarthy recalls the case of a couple who actually drew a line through the house, with each agreeing to stay in their own half while settlement discussions were still under way. A parody of this can be seen in the 1989 film *The War of the Roses*, starring Michael Douglas and Kathleen Turner, with Danny DeVito as the family lawyer.

McCarthy goes on to say that "if a couple decides the best thing is for one party to temporarily vacate the house, leaving the kids behind … [that will be] extremely prejudicial to the person moving out."

Children are usually caught in the crossfire of their parents' marital battles, becoming the chief casualties of the divorce. Parents often use them to heal their own bruised egos, or they vie for the children's favour. The children are thus forced into a conflict of loyalties. More often than not the struggle wreaks havoc on their developing personalities.

The most devastating court battle is the custody proceeding. The judge, with his or her wide discretionary powers, becomes a referee between the warring parties. Experience has shown that the effects of court custody decisions do not so much terminate the dispute as give them a new form. The battle for custody becomes the battle for visitation rights.

Most often, one parent is given custody; the other is given visitation rights. If bitterness still exists between the parents — and it often does — the new arguments tend to focus on visitation. The non-custodial parent may not be able to accept the judge's decision. He or she may create special problems by not picking the children up on time, or by bringing them back late. The custodial parent may then have a lawyer send off an affidavit to the effect that the non-custodial parent has violated the visitation terms. The parent with custody feels the other parent's behaviour harms the children. He or she wants to prevent the other parent from seeing the children altogether. The cycle begins again. Old wounds are reopened and the parents and children return to court before another judge with yet another unresolved issue.

The continuing bitterness may result in one legal battle after another. The parties may become so paralyzed by their continuing struggle that they are unable to begin building new lives. In essence, the adversary system has led the parents to become litigation junkies with their respective lawyers helping supply them with ammunition. The children become property to be fought over and divided. Great emotional damage is done to everyone.

Justice Harvey Brownstone, writing in his recent book *Tug of War*, makes these two points:

1. Be child-focused. Parents must learn to love their children more than they dislike each other.
2. Consider mediation before giving the decision-making power to a judge. With the right help, you and your ex-partner may be able to arrive at compromises that will be better for your family than a court-imposed decision.[7]

M. Patrician captures the heightened atmosphere of custody hearings with her new take on an old poem:

'Twas the night before court, when all through the house,
Not a creature was peaceful, not even a mouse.
Depositions and petitions were spread all over the floor,
And each parent was hopeful of winning the custody war.
The minor children were restless, huddled under their beds,
While visions of judges haunted their little heads.
The attorneys, with their closing arguments memorized,
Plotted and planned to crack the other parent's lies.
Then they settled their brains for a long heated court battle....[8]

Judge Paula J. Hepner comments on the effects litigation has on children:

What little civility is left between two parents before walking into court is almost always destroyed by their posturing in the litigation. However, the only information parents will present is a list of their injustices portraying each other in the worst possible light: the most abusive, the most irresponsible, the most uninvolved, the most inconsiderate, the most immoral, the most inadequate, the most controlling, the most ... the most. Indeed the majority of parents view the case as their chance to get their day in court when, in actuality, it is their *children's* day in court.[9]

I, too, have found similar parents who get caught up in the adversary system and are blind to how the process is hurting their children. Clearly, a custody hearing before the judge is simply a legal lottery with no winners.

This battle also sometimes involves one of the saddest realities of adversary divorce: parental alienation, in which parents try to turn the children against the other parent. If you can avoid the following list of wilful behaviours, you will take a giant step toward protecting your children from the fallout of your divorce.

Destructive Conduct That Could Harm the Relationship with Your Children and Former Partner

1. Putting down the other parent.
2. Accusing the other parent.
3. Don't let it be the child's decision when to see the other parent, when there is an agreement to see the other parent.
4. Imposing your parenting rules in the other parent's home.

5. Arguing with the other parent in front of the children.
6. Encouraging the child to be disrespectful to the other parent.
7. Making the child feel guilty when he goes to the other parent.
8. Telling your child the details of the legal proceedings, and why the marriage came to an end.
9. Involving the children in play activities just before the child is going to the other parents home.
10. Returning the child to the other parent when late, or early and not notifying the other parent.

Tragically, these tactics work. In fact, they can even cause children to become alienated from *both* parents.

I recently had a case that clearly identified a situation of parental alienation. The husband had left his wife for a woman who was a neighbour and friend to both him and his wife. When his wife found out about the affair, she became extremely angry and forbid her husband to see his eight-year-old son. The case was then referred to me to see if I could resolve the parenting issue. After interviewing both parents, I felt it was important for me to see their son, James, for an individual session.

James was extremely anxious and he had a difficult time looking at me and answering my questions other than in mono-syllabic phrases. When I asked him why he wasn't seeing his dad, he said in clear and angry tones, "Why should I, he divorced me and my mom?" I then asked what he meant by "divorced him," and he further related to me that his mother had told him on several occasions that his father had divorced both he and his mother. The situation was clearly leading to one of parental alienation and had to be referred on to a parenting coordinator who specialized in situations of parental alienation.

It should be noted that couples involved in cases of alienation such as the one described above cannot stay in the mediation process. They should be referred to an agency for counselling or therapy and perhaps to litigation follow-ing a court assessment. Clearly, these cases are not able to be mediated.

THE INSANITY OF HIGH-CONFLICT DIVORCE

Consider the case of a family I dealt with in my practice.

Let's call the couple Bob and Susan Morrow. This couple started off in a reasonable, low-conflict divorce through medi-ation. However, they eventually gave in to the seductive power of the adversary system, which played on their emotional issues and offered them false hope that someone could win.

To their friends, this couple's marriage seemed as good as a modern marriage could be. Though by no means wealthy, they were financially comfortable. They were both intelligent and committed to each other. Bob was a successful architect who worked on several major corporate projects. Susan was a skilled executive secretary in a brokerage house. Their joint income was sufficient to support a suburban townhouse, two cars, and a good school for their two children. They had prob-lems, of course, but the couple was secure in their ability to solve them.

At first both were interested in succeeding in their careers for the benefit of the family as a whole. But as competition grew heavier in their respective workplaces and their indi-vidual careers grew more demanding, they gradually began to grow apart. They developed separate goals and separate friendships. They admitted to each other that their needs were diverging.

At the beginning of their marriage and through the years of the birth of their children, Bob and Susan had genuinely liked and respected each other. But as they began to develop separate interests and identities, they became bored with their relationship. Boredom alternated with frenzied attempts to recapture the old urgency, but the romance had disappeared. They tried various experiments, including separate vacations, marital counselling, and even individual psychotherapy. But nothing seemed to work.

The only logical alternative, it seemed to them, was a friendly divorce in which no one would be unduly damaged, especially the children. Separately, they consulted their surprised friends for the names of lawyers who might help.

During this period the Morrows maintained a facade of understanding. However, as their relationship unravelled and became more and more superficial, the children began to show the strain. This was clear from the classroom behaviour of their daughter, Alice, now thirteen years old. Alice's teacher noted the child's dramatic shift of mood. She had become practically non-communicative, shied away from her friends, and seemed lonely and depressed. The school psychologist, after assessing her, reported that Alice was reacting to an unhappy home situation.

Susan's lawyer suggested that she sue for custody and a liberal maintenance settlement. Bob's lawyer suggested that he recover a major portion of the property. The Morrows had officially entered the downward spiral of destructive conflict inherent in the adversary system. From this point on, they themselves would have to assume the role of adversaries. The chances of any co-operation diminished as threats and counterthreats mounted through their lawyers' letters and affidavits.

When Bob's lawyer first contacted him with news of Susan's intentions to file for a divorce, he was not surprised. He was surprised by Susan's affidavit. In it she swore, as grounds for divorce, to an incident proving mental cruelty. Bob could not believe his ears when his lawyer read these words from the affidavit: "My husband stood in front of me naked, all the while telling me how he wanted to sleep with my friend, Diane, and what he would do with her."

The affidavit, his lawyer explained during their meeting, was a public record that might be used in court.

Bob tried to recall the circumstances. His frank response to his lawyer was, "Well, I probably did say that I found Diane sexually attractive, but I never meant it in the way she said I did."

It didn't take much encouragement from his counsel for Bob to file his own affidavit in response to the humiliating damage caused by the details in his wife's affidavit. He swore in his papers that his wife was an unfit mother who mistreated the children, leaving them alone and exposing them to her own sexual misconduct.

In a saner time, Bob and Susan would have reacted quite differently. Susan would have admitted that both she and her husband had discussed their desire for other partners. Bob would have said that the one time Susan had left the kids alone had been years ago when she went to borrow something from a neighbour.

But the Morrows were not living in a sane time. They were now officially involved in the insanity of high-conflict divorce.

On the advice of her lawyer, Susan moved out of their bedroom and slept on the studio couch in the den. He advised this and other courses of action to influence her husband to move out of the house. She was not entirely convinced that this was proper behaviour, but she was afraid if she didn't go on the offensive, Bob might get custody of the children.

Bob's reaction was predictable. He began staying late at the office. His occasional glass of wine became less occasional. He sought feminine companionship to shore up his damaged ego.

Meanwhile, the collateral damage began to be felt. Letters were sent back and forth between family members. The in-laws, who had always been friendly with one another, sided with their respective children. The entire family and social network that had grown up around the marriage was shattered as everyone took sides.

Closer to the scene of battle, Bob and Susan made it clear to their children that the other parent was responsible for the marital breakdown. Each parent competed for the love and support of the kids by giving them expensive presents and trips.

The children's sadness revealed itself at school. Naturally, this became more cannon fodder for the marital battle. Each parent blamed the other for the children's behaviour. Each began to openly demean and undermine the other in front of the children.

During the course of the Morrows' divorce, friends, relatives and even the couple's children were interrogated and cross-examined. Bob and Susan each pressed an "expert witness" into service.

In the case of the Morrows, separate marriage counsellors acted as expert witnesses. Sometimes psychiatrists are used. It's worth noting here that role of the expert witness is, in fact, contradictory. Far from being an impartial witness in possession of specialized factual information, this person is present only to promote his or her client or patient's case. The expert witness and the lawyer form a team. The other side, of course, has its own team. Neither one of the expert witnesses has ever interviewed the other spouse. Each, however, makes claims and counterclaims about the suitability of his client or patient and the unsuitability of the other partner.

Unfortunately, cases like the Morrows' can end up going back to court even after the judge has ruled on the case. Why? Because the language used in this process itself contributes to the unresolved nature of the litigation. For example, the fact that custody is awarded to the "winner" as if the child or children were a prize, is discouraging.

I WON, WE LOST

So, what was the result of the Morrows' bitter struggle? Bob lost his children, Susan was financially ruined, both of their careers suffered, and their children required extended therapy.

The lawyers, courts, and the system, meanwhile, could be satisfied that all avenues of destructive confrontation had been used in finalizing the divorce. After all, true to the adversarial nature of the divorce process, there were winners and losers. In the eyes of the legal system, Susan was the winner. She won custody of the children. Bob was the loser. He lost his children. If he was lucky, he'd get some "access" to them. It is implied, of course, that the loser was "at fault." After all, this is what the adversary system is all about.

But in truth, no matter which member of the couple wins legally, both lose. A host of other people lose, too. The members of the extended family didn't ask for a divorce, yet in reality they are now severed from heretofore close relationships. And the biggest losers are the children. They are often used as pawns by their parents to salvage their own bruised egos — or to bruise their partner's ego. The children are forced into a conflict of loyalties that more often than not damages their developing personalities. It's no surprise that kids get caught in the conflict when, as Roman and Haddad put it, "Marriage failure plus grief, minus social approval multiplied by emotional distress and divided by low self-esteem, equals depression, anxiety, perhaps panic, and the behaviour that these emotions elicit."[10]

I came across the following story by accident, and yet appropriately, when I was studying mediation in Los Angeles at the beginning of my career:

Biologists Watch in Horror:
Condors Squabble, Destroy Precious Egg

VENTURA (UPI) — The only California condor egg known to have been laid this breeding season has been destroyed by its parents, who knocked it off a cliff while fighting over which bird should take care of the rare egg.

A team of specialists trying to save the huge, endangered birds watched in horror as the precious egg smashed on the rocks below the condors' cave and was eaten by scavenging ravens.

"There was real musical chairs going on in the nest," said the co-director of the program to save the huge vultures, which have wing spreads of up to twelve feet.

"One of them would sit down on the egg and the other would come in and try to push the first one off," he said. "They would jab each other in the face and really get physical."

Biologists with the condor program, which is operated jointly by the federal Fish and Wildlife Service and the National Audubon Society, said team members observed the pair during the past several weeks while they were engaged in courtship manoeuvres.

One member of the team saw the mother condor lay the egg, the only one known to have been produced this season.

The scientists were delighted because the addition of even one bird to the minuscule condor population — estimated at only 25 to 30 birds — would represent a significant improvement in the species' chances for survival.

The birds had chosen a cave in the side of the steep cliff in the foothills surrounding Ventura for their nest.

46

But almost immediately, the parents began to bicker over "incubation and rights" to the egg.

At one point, the co-director of the program said, the quarrelling became so furious that both birds took to the air and started squawking and flailing at each other with their wings and talons, leaving the egg unattended.

"This went on for hours," he lamented. "They were so absorbed no one was incubating."

The scientists observed the fighting from a blind about a half-mile away, but there was nothing they could do to help settle the dispute. The bickering got worse and about a week ago, and as the parents were pushing and shoving inside the cave, the four-inch egg suddenly was knocked out of the nest toward the cave entrance.

It teetered on the lip of the cave, then fell to a rock ledge below, where its contents were rapidly devoured by the ravens.

The similarity between couples who become caught up in high-conflict behaviour and these condors is all too great.

CAUGHT IN THE MIDDLE

In the case of one family I dealt with, a twelve-year-old boy was unable to see his father on his scheduled weekend visit. When the father finally was able to visit him some weeks later, he encouraged the boy not to return to his mother. When the boy visited my office, he pleaded with me to stop his parents from hurting him. His words described the classic double bind: "If I agree with Mom, Dad gets mad at me, and when I agree with Dad, Mom gets mad. I think if they got back together, things would be a lot better."

Newly separated parents, in the midst of dealing with a sense of loss and isolation, need a great deal of support and energy to cope with their children. Resentment is often forthcoming on the part of the non-custodial parent. At the same time, the parent with custody may take revenge on the other parent by denying access to the children.

Even when both parents are aware of these dangers and make a conscious effort to prevent them, their own high level of anxiety throughout the entire divorce process weakens their parenting abilities. When the parents mentioned above were confronted with what they were doing to their son, they were unable to appreciate how they were hurting the child because they were so preoccupied with putting each other down. They wanted to cast their son as the judge. Each blamed the other for the terrible situation. Each produced affidavits from their opposing lawyers denouncing each other's ability to parent.

The outcome of this and similar situations is a "revolving courtroom door." Years after the court decision, families still find themselves going back to court and fighting over other legal issues.

Here, for example, is a letter written by a divorced father to his son, who remained in his mother's custody. The father is so bitter about the marriage breakup that he is blind to the effects of his harmful words on his son:

Dear Mark,

Well, we finally made it. Your brother Bill and I have been lying on the beach here in sunny California. Only one thing is missing and that's you, big fella! If mom wasn't so mean and trying her best to keep us apart, you'd be here with us. Bill mentioned to me when we were leaving Disneyland the other night, how sad it made him feel that you couldn't be with us.

48

When we come back, I'm going to ask my lawyer
if he can help me to get you to come and live with us.
I know it will be difficult, but it's the only way that
we can stop your mom from keeping us apart. With
all the legal bills she made me pay, it's really going to
be hard on Bill and me, but your wonderful grand-
mother has offered to lend me the money to help pay
the legal bills. I hope your mother knows what she is
doing to us, and that someday soon we will win out
and she will know what it's like to suffer the way we
are now. The next time you see the shrink, make sure
you tell him how unhappy you are, and how much you
want to come and live with us.

When you say your prayers, ask God to help
reunite us.

Will call you next week. God bless.

Love, Dad and Brother Bill

Clearly, the fathers intent was strictly a manipulation of
his child which suggests a path towards parental alienation.

In my practice, I have seen some children develop low
self-esteem as a result of their parents' conflictual behaviour.
If their parents no longer love each other the way they once
did, will they be the next to lose that love? The divorce introduces a frightening thought to children, who depend on the
love of their parents: that love can die.

The best way to help your children is to learn how to cope
yourself. You have to let go of the past and have a positive
approach, by making a new life as a single parent and building on your own self-esteem. This will enable you to give your
children the kind of support and direction that they will need.
This should help you to show your children lots of understanding and patience. Practise active listening and give them
guidance and firmness. Above all, build a firewall between

your marital problems and your children. Fix firmly in your mind and heart that they do not deserve to be casualties of your marital conflicts.

Try not to play the blame game: "It doesn't matter whose idea the divorce is. There is no point in blaming the one who wants out. You can't make someone love you and you can't stop a divorce. There is no point in making things worse than by fighting what is. Once you stop struggling and accept the inevitable, you actually feel more at peace. So there is the choice, are you going to lawyer up and fight or are you going to be smart and work together?"[11]

I often use the following metaphor to illustrate the importance of letting go of feelings resulting in the end of a marriage:

> In a jungle there lived a troupe of monkeys. These monkeys were much like all others except that they loved to eat a particular local fruit. When the local villagers stumbled upon this fact, they devised a means of capturing the monkeys to add them to the local zoo. They built wooden traps that resembled birdcages. They built the bars of these cages so that a determined monkey could insert his hand into the trap to grab a piece of fruit but could remove his hand only by letting go of the aphrodisiac.
>
> The villagers eventually captured many of the monkeys, for even when the monkeys saw a villager coming at them with a net, their love of the fruit was so great that rather than relinquish it and escape, they submitted to capture.

WHAT YOU NEED TO KNOW ABOUT
THE ADVERSARY SYSTEM

Responsible members of the legal profession freely admit that the adversary system, including so-called uncontested divorce, does not function to anyone's benefit save the lawyers who make a substantial living from destructive conflict. Such lawyers are few in number, but significant nonetheless. Some of them are in the vanguard of trying to reform family law. Their aim is to make the adversary approach a last, and not a first, resort.

The role played by some lawyers who find themselves caught in the adversarial system may worsen the relationship between spouses and increase the negative impact on their children.

> It is possible for lawyers to negotiate too hard. In pursuit of the best possible agreement for their clients, some lawyers seem to worsen the post-marital relationship of their client and the client's spouse. They may, for example, actively discourage a client from talking with his or her spouse for fear that the client will inadvertently weaken his or her negotiating position, or will, in thoughtless generosity, make concessions without obtaining anything in return. Or, they may take positions more extreme than their client desires in order to achieve an advantageous compromise, but by so doing they are apt to anger the client's spouse and further alienate the spouse from the client. Some separated individuals reported that until negotiations were at an end, their relationship with their spouse became progressively worse.[12]

CHILDREN COME FIRST

THE BAD OLD DAYS

The role of the divorce attorney as an adversary is described by Herbert Glieberman in his book, *Confessions of a Divorce Lawyer.* "There's only one rule on divorce settlement: if you represent the wife, get as much as possible; if you represent the husband, give away as little as possible."

The author goes on to say, "Now, as I walk through the outer door of my office heading for the courtroom, I know that I'm walking to a case where there will be no compromises, no mediations, no good feelings to balance the bad. This will be an all-out confrontation, a real tooth and nail fight. I'll love it. Now, finally we're here. And it's a real circus. The other side has two accountants, a tax lawyer, three expert witnesses and a defendant; our side has one accountant, a comptroller, no tax lawyers because I've become expert at that, and seven expert witnesses."[13]

Although a number of years have passed since Glieberman wrote his book, and many lawyers have moved forward in advocating mediation and other forms of dispute resolution, some still function in the traditional adversarial partisan role.

Most of us believe that lawyers do not deal with the emotional content of their cases, that they take a "just the facts" approach. Not true. It is remarkable how easily lawyers get drawn into the fracas, ratcheting up their efforts to win the case for their client. Or, in contrast, how easy it is for them to become compassionate and concerned for their own or both clients. There are many conciliatory divorce lawyers, but they are hampered by the very existence of an adversary system that permits a tough attorney to "walk all over them." For example, when a lawyer does take the children's interest to heart and attempts to use conciliatory methods through negotiation, he or she may worsen the situation for the children by becoming easy prey for the lawyer on the other side.

It is not the fault of individual lawyers; the adversary system in family law simply puts them into a process in which it's difficult to bring about the required resolutions, such as promoting parental co-operation and good will, and encouraging parents to accept mutual responsibility for their children by helping them formulate clear and specific parenting plans in their children's best interest.

It should be noted that mediators themselves sometimes have difficulty in the roles they play out with families who come to mediation. For example, some mediators are really conducting custody assessments when they are in a position to write reports that determine custody and access issues. It is my belief that confidentiality should be an important part of the mediation process. Otherwise, clients cast mediators in the role of judges and it is very difficult to get honest disclosure under those conditions. Be careful when hiring a mediator to make sure that confidentiality and privilege is stated clearly in the mediation contract.

Furthermore, it is important to ask the mediator if he or she is certified under state or provincial regulations as a family mediator. Certified family mediators have to meet important professional standards to provide a certain degree of competence. It's very critical that a mediator serves as a facilitator or catalyst, not an authoritarian, within the mediation process. Your mediator should become involved in the dispute resolution process only to enable or empower you to discover your own solution.

Divorce mediation helps lawyers on both sides to heed their better instincts because it requires both lawyers to be conciliatory. Today, mediators are working with collaborative lawyer teams in order to avoid unnecessary litigation. Clearly, there is a place for litigation; however, it should be utilized when appropriate. It should follow mediation that has broken down, or when mediation is not appropriate. Once again, it should be noted that both parties should have independent legal representation while in the process of mediation.

3

How Divorce Mediation Protects Children

Every missile you send to your ex-spouse goes through the heart of your children.

Once you've made the decision to separate, it's important for you to have a plan that protects your children from the traumatic experiences described in the previous chapter. Your mediator will actually coach you in helping your children cope.

HOW AND WHAT TO TELL THE CHILDREN

The way you and your spouse handle the divorce is the most important factor in helping your children. This starts with how you tell your children about the divorce.

- If possible, don't tell them until you have clear plans on what you are doing, when you are going to separate, who they will be staying with, and if there are going to be any changes.

- It's better if you both tell the children together and tell all the children at the same time. Pick a place where they are comfortable and with little distractions.
- Also, pick a time of the day that will allow them time to absorb what is being said and allows them time to ask questions.
- Be careful not to say anything negative about the other parent or how the marriage ended, no matter how your personal feelings may be getting in the way. The result would be devastating and have long lasting negative effects for your children.
- Acknowledge your child's sadness and let them know that it's okay to feel this way. Let them know that they can talk with you any time and ask any questions.
- Before one of you moves out of the home, you should allow at least a week or two from the time you tell the children until the actual move. This gives the children time to talk to each of their parents and gives you time to reassure them that everything is going to be all right.
- Basically, you want them to understand that now they will have two homes instead of one.
- You want to do your best to keep the kids in the same school they are attending.
- Reassure your children that they will always be protected and helped going through this difficult time.
- Discipline yourself to remember the good parts of your marriage with your children.
- It is critical to make sure that your children do not blame themselves for the divorce.

If I were to ask you what job number one is for parents, you would probably say to give the kids your love and to protect them from harm. This job does not disappear for you as parents once you have decided to separate. Use divorce mediation as a way to continue loving and protecting your children.

YOUR CHILDREN DESERVE BETTER

The following principles that flow from mediation will help you to avoid conflict that can hurt your children. I give these principles to all of my clients after my first session with them.

- Children of divorce do best in the short and long run when they **feel loved and cared for by both parents**. This is most likely to occur when the children have ongoing contact with both parents who participate fully in their lives. Children feel more secure and better about themselves knowing both parents want them and want to be involved in their lives, and it helps diminish feelings of abandonment and rejection. Children also need consistency and stability. The children's need for frequent contact and for stability must be adjusted to arrive at a healthy balance. This balance will depend on many factors, including those related to the children the parents, and the circumstances.
- Most children in divorced families struggle to some extent with a **loyalty bind**, that is, they feel torn when their commitment to one parent may be seen as disloyalty to the other parent. How this manifests is related to many factors, including the children's age, their developmental levels, their temperament, and their academic, social, and emotional adjustment. Be sure you don't exacerbate this fear by actually vying for their loyalty to you over the other parent.
- Children adjust better when they have each parent's implicit and explicit permission and acceptance to have a relationship with the other parent. Parents should acknowledge the relevance of the other parent to their children's lives.

- The children's overall adjustment and their relationship with both parents will be compromised if they are exposed to disapproving attitudes or negative comments about the other parent; and/or if one parent undermines the other (even when he or she thinks the other parent deserves it). This applies when the children may be in the vicinity, playing in the other room, or "probably asleep." Parents should also not allow any other person to denigrate the other parent in front of the children. Parents are advised to refer to any differences between situations or homes as "differences," not as "better" or "worse" conditions.

- The children have been exposed to such denigration when one parent blames the other for the divorce, or undermines the other with derogatory comments, or is critical of the other's lifestyle or personality. When this occurs, the children will have difficulty showing that they are happy spending time with the other parent, as this would only let their present parent down. In an effort to cope, the children may say things to each parent that they think they want or need to hear. These comments may be distortions, exaggerations, or even untruths said to appease or ingratiate themselves to their parents, such as not enjoying an outing, having only eaten junk food, having stayed up very late, and other misrepresentations or exaggerations of what a parent allowed or said or did.

- If one parent finds that what the children have said is of significant concern, that parent should first ask the other parent what actually happened in a nonjudgmental way. Also, children who are repeatedly caught in a loyalty bind become masters of manipulation. For example, they learn to play one parent off against the other. Often, the result is that the children lose respect for both parents. If a complaint is made to one parent about the other, the children should be encouraged to talk directly to the parent they are complaining about.

- Further, each parent should respect the other's privacy and not ask the children questions about the other parent's personal life or activities. Rather, showing a casual interest in the children's activities is important for the children's self-esteem. At the same time, the parents are wise to recognize the difference between open-ended casual questions of interest and pointed and repeated questioning. Casual questioning includes such questions as, "How are you?" "How did you enjoy your time?" or "What did you do that was fun?" as well as picking up on the children's spontaneous statements. Pointed questioning includes such questions as, "Where did you go?" "Who was that?" or "How long did you stay?" Although the parent may be genuinely interested, pointed questions tend to put undue pressure on the children and may hamper their adjustment.

- The negative effect on inter-parental conflict on child adjustment has been well-documented. Every missile we send to our ex-spouse goes through the heart of our child(ren). Observing parents verbally mistreating each other communicates to the children that their parents do not respect or like each other. This message exacerbates the children's loyalty bind and negatively affects all aspects of their adjustment. Healthy child adjustment requires parental co-operation, mutual respect, and the absence of parental conflict. Any discussions between the parents during transition times must be limited to brief and cordial exchanges. The parents are wise to work toward establishing a "business" relationship with each other for the sake of the children.

- Regular meetings and/or telephone calls should be arranged. If these are impossible or ineffective, the parents need to communicate in writing or through a third party. Financial matters should not be discussed in front of the children. Co-operative parenting is best for healthy child adjustment. If the parents cannot remain amicable, it is better for them to remain disengaged than to expose the children to conflict.

- It will damage the children's current and future adjustment if they are relied on to carry messages (including support cheques) between the parents. It is imperative that the parents not rely on the children for communication. If the children ask either parent for a change in the time-sharing schedule, the parent is advised to say that the parents will discuss the matter, decide if they can accommodate the request, and get back to the children.

- Difficulties with transitions and with "settling back down" after time with the other parent are to be expected. While these adjustments are due, in part, to the children's exposure to different routines and different child management styles, difficulties at transition times have less to do with the children's experience of the other parent and more to do with the transition itself and with their parents' conduct. Parents are advised to examine their role in the children's difficulties with transitions and with "settling in." If one parent undermines the other, even covertly, as described above, the children may show disrespect for and test the limits with the undermined parent. These parent-child conflicts (which to some extent are normal) will influence the children's ability to re-settle into the routines upon re-entering the undermined parent's home. Most children will come to adjust to differences in routines and lifestyles between their parents.

The parent's sensitivity to the children's predicament and loyalty bind is critical at transition times. Coming down hard on children to quickly resume usual routines is unlikely to be as effective as a combination of empathy, flexibility, and firmness.

CHILDREN'S SENSE OF LOSS

It's important for you to look at your children's experience in relation to your separation or divorce. The most common reaction is a sense of loss as they become aware that one of their parents will no longer be living in the family home. Often the children's sense of loss can result in feelings of confusion and anxiety. In my practice, I have found that some children will look for ways to reunify their parents. Some will feign illness, act out at school, and essentially take on the role of scapegoat in order to get their parents back together again. Many children feel that a conflictual home is better than not knowing what is going to happen to them in the future.

It's not unusual for older children to try to become a partner with the residential parent, essentially taking on the role of the absent parent. Parents having their own issues to deal with may feed into the problem by giving the children too much authority, or in fact, too much responsibility.

Finally, your children may begin to test the new situation. They can play one parent off against the other in an attempt to deal with some of their own insecurities.

Above all, be careful what you say. Children seldom misquote you. In fact, they usually repeat word for word what you shouldn't have said.

61

CHILDREN COME FIRST

DON'T GET EVEN, GET EQUAL

How can divorcing parents relate to each other in ways that protect their children? How can they avoid collateral damage resulting from conflictual behaviours where children get caught in the middle?

Mediation can help parents develop the will and discipline to avoid the trap of desiring a win for themselves over a win for the whole family. Mediation does not attempt to solve the unsolvable; most mediators will refuse to debate "who did what" during the marriage. The emphasis of mediation, instead, is on *both parents sharing responsibility for their children*. Indeed, research shows that children benefit from the meaningful involvement of both parents. The emphasis is on *both*.

AVOIDING THE USUAL POWER STRUGGLES

The way we see things can determine the outcome. For instance, long-term suffering follows in the wake of a conflict that is seen as a fight to the finish in which anything goes if it serves to help a party win. We would do better to think of conflict the way the Chinese do. The closest word they have for conflict is made up of two symbols, one meaning "danger" and the other "opportunity." It is possible for conflict to be constructive when it is looked at in this way.

Conflict escalates when

- other people become involved in the dispute and take sides.
- one or both of you feel threatened.
- there is no interest or investment in maintaining the relationship.

- there is a history of unproductive, negative conflict between you and your partner.
- there is an increase in the acting out of anger, fear, or frustration.
- important needs involved are not acknowledged and met.
- there is a lack of the skills necessary for peacemaking.

A conflict de-escalates when

- you and your partner focus on the problem rather than on each other.
- you create a safe place where your emotions of anger, fear, and frustration may be expressed directly rather than demonstrated indirectly.
- threats are reduced or eliminated.
- needs are allowed to be openly discussed.
- already existing skills in conflict resolution and negotiation are built upon and used.[14]

Divorce mediation can resolve conflict by helping you

- understand the subtext of your unresolved conflict.
- make the transition from marital roles and relations to your parental roles and relations.
- block or change patterns of conduct that are likely to interfere with productive negotiation in mediation.
- resolve any feelings of anger you have toward your former partner.
- reframe divorce in positive terms, that is, as a form of family reorganization that affords members an opportunity for a new beginning, and for personal and/or family transformation.

A REASONABLE FIRST ALTERNATIVE

Parents, children, lawyers, judges, the system, and society all gain when co-operative methods are used instead of destructive ones.

We will always need a legal structure that allows people to "have their day in court" when no other method satisfies them. But the most extreme solution should be the last solution to be tried, not the first. This is where divorce mediation comes in. Divorce mediation shows quite conclusively that destructive confrontation is not necessary for the vast majority of divorcing couples.

In fact, you should beware that only 15 percent of divorce cases go to court. What they're *not* saying is that it may take many months and years and thousands of dollars to get to the point where the settlement is made.

The following situation illustrates how some couples choose mediation when they realize how destructive high-conflict divorce coupled with the adversary system can be to their children.

John spoke to me after six months of spending a great deal of money in a custody battle for his daughter, Emma. His wife, Linda, had hired an aggressive lawyer, and he hired an equally aggressive one to match hers.

Now he wondered if there was a better way. I coached him in putting together a letter to his wife. Here's what he wrote:

Dear Linda,

In the interests of a brighter future for our daughter, Emma, I want to apologize for prolonging this conflict between us. If the conflict continues, it will get only worse for our daughter. And for us. I am writing to express that I want to discuss Emma with you openly and without hostility to see if you and I can make some decisions directly — without going through lawyers.

Please accept my apology for the mistakes I made that led to this divorce and all the trouble we've been through. I wish I could take back the wrong things I did. I acknowledge my mistakes. We share a lifetime responsibility. The beautiful daughter we created and whom we both love deserves the best that both of us can give her.

I believe we have a choice: squander our emotional and financial resources and risk the future of our daughter, or sit down together and figure out a way to work together for the sake of our daughter.

Would you consider with me the possibility of counselling and mediation in order to build and agree on a working relationship, rather than leaving it to the courts to determine all of our futures?

Let me know if you are open to this. Let's get together to discuss our options, without prejudice of course.

Sincerely,
John

And here's how Linda replied:

John,

No apologies necessary. My goal has been to protect Emma, but I can see that the legal process has actually put her in jeopardy. She needs our committed care. She needs to see her parents in responsible, consistent, adult roles.

She will benefit from our efforts to cooperate. However, in case things do not work out in our attempts to come to an outside-the-court parenting agreement, I think we should continue on to the next steps required by the legal system we are currently involved in.

Furthermore, to confirm your commitment to sharing responsibility for parenting Emma, it would be appreciated if you would pay the support as ordered by the court.

I am grateful to see from your letter that you recognize the financial and emotional duress you have put me in. It has been stressful beyond belief for me to care for Emma while having to defend her right to be supported by you.

I, too, welcome the opportunity to end the legal and financial madness. I look forward to discussing with you the way forward for our daughter.

Sincerely,
Linda

No one "wins" when using divorce mediation. Nonetheless, everyone benefits.

MEDIATION CAN LESSEN THE NEGATIVE EFFECTS OF DIVORCE ON CHILDREN

A number of studies point to the fact that many children develop low self-esteem as a result of their parents' divorce. The children are described as being terribly worried that the remaining parent will also leave, and that the child will feel that he is going to be orphaned. Some studies have mentioned the questioning attitude of children. If their parents who once loved each other no longer do, will they be the next to lose that love? The divorce introduces the idea that love can die. For the child who depends on the love of his or her parents, this can be a frightening thought.

This clearly points to the need for divorce mediation to help families adjust to the divorce in a way that will lead to families co-operating in resolving conflict rather than engaging in a pattern of destructive or contentious behaviour. The question of how the separation and divorce is handled, as opposed to the breakdown itself, is of great importance.

It isn't always so destructive for children when their parents separate. Children who are exposed to high-conflict intact families will have a more difficult time than those children whose parents divorce and are amicable and supportive of each other.

A BILL OF RIGHTS FOR CHILDREN

In an attempt to decrease the high-conflict approach to divorce, the family court of Milwaukee has devised the following Bill of Rights for Children in Divorce Actions. Adhering to this Bill of Rights will help you keep your children out of harm's way. The bill states that children are entitled to the following rights:

1. The right to be treated as an interested and affected person and not as a pawn, possession or chattel of either or both parents.
2. The right to grow to maturity in that home environment which will best guarantee an opportunity for the child to grow to mature and responsible citizenship.

3. The right to the day by day love, care, discipline and protection of the parent having custody of the child.
4. The right to know the non-custodial parent and to have the benefit of such parent's love and guidance through adequate visitations.
5. The right to a positive and constructive relationship with both parents, with neither parent to be permitted to degrade or downgrade the other in the mind of the child.
6. The right to have moral and ethical values developed by precept and practices and have limits set for behaviour so that the child early in life may develop self-discipline and self-control.
7. The right to the most adequate level of economic support that can be provided by the best efforts of both parents.
8. The right to the same opportunities for education that the child would have had if the family unit had not been broken.
9. The right to periodic review of custodial arrangements and child support orders as the circumstances of the parents and the benefit of the child may require.
10. The right to recognition that children involved in a divorce are always disadvantaged parties and that the law must take affirmative steps to protect their welfare, including, where indicated, a social investigation to determine, and the appointment of a guardian *ad litem*, to protect their interests.[15]

A MEDIATED DIVORCE FROM A
CHILD'S POINT OF VIEW

This section is written for young people whose parents are contemplating separation or divorce or whose families have already separated. Generally, it is intended for those over the age of thirteen, but if you have younger brothers or sisters you might wish to read it and then talk to them about some of the ideas presented.

Reading this material is not going to solve all your problems or end what you are going through. It will explain what may occur, how you are going to be involved, and where you can find someone with whom you can discuss your own personal problems. Every divorce case is different because the people involved are individuals, because the laws vary from place to place, and because no two situations are exactly alike.

Let's start with honesty. You love both of your parents and you really want them to stay together. The chances are, however, that you can't help them get back together. But you can help to make things easier both for them and for yourself.

This year, more than one million people will get divorced. Many more will become separated or try what is called a "trial separation." This may be terribly difficult for the children because children often feel that they must choose between their parents.

It is a time of confusion and mixed emotions. Many questions arise — unfortunately, they are questions that are extremely difficult to answer. One common question is: "How can two people fall out of love? And, who is to blame for divorce?"

As you know, the love that two adults feel for one another is quite different than the love they feel for their children. People who live together usually experience periods of tension. Sometimes they resolve their difficulties, sometimes the tensions grow worse and the couple decides to part company. People who fall out of love with one another go on loving their children; it is important for you to realize this.

Let's have a closer look at some of the questions you may be asking.

Who's to blame for divorce? Now, let's think about why this question is being asked in the first place. Does it matter? This is the question you may want to ask because you may think it will help you make some kind of choice, if indeed you have to make a choice. It is also the question the legal system may ask. Our legal system as it is presently set up is, unhappily, designed to "find fault" — to find out who is to blame. But, legal definitions of "fault" do not often apply to human relationships. When people are involved in getting a separation and divorce they are often angry with each other. They blame each other and say and do things that they would not do under normal circumstances. When you ask, "Who's to blame?" you may really be saying "Am I to blame?" or "Which parent should I choose?"

It is not necessary for you to choose which parent you love the most. You probably love them both equally. As for the unspoken question, "Am I to blame?" the answer is no. The answer is no even if you are sometimes the focus of your parents' arguments. People who are deeply angry with one another may fight over the way coffee is prepared or how one of them is treating you. Not all people who are angry fight, of course. Some of them simply cease speaking to one another and fill rooms with sullen silence. In either case, you must realize that you are not the cause of their problems. In other words, it is not so important to know who is to blame as it is for you to realize you are *not* to blame.

If you have younger brothers and sisters, they might be afraid. They may wonder if your mother and father, who have fallen out of love with one another, could fall out of love with them, too. You can help reassure them that this won't happen.

The next important question is: **What can I do?** Earlier, it was indicated that you probably can't help solve your parents' problems. If you plead with them to stay together you may only make them feel guiltier. Guilt is not a healthy basis for family life. Look around you! You probably have many friends whose parents don't get along well, but who still live together. The chances are that their family life is disturbing and that they complain they can't communicate with their parents.

Having parents who are separated or divorced is probably not as bad as it sounds, especially if you can maintain a good relationship with them. There are a few simple things you can do to ensure a good future relationship. First, do not take sides. Talk to your parents together and tell them that you love them both and that you are not giving up your relationship with either of them. One or both of your parents may try to "win" you over to their side. They may try to talk about the other parent to you. People in a highly emotional state do this because they need support, but it can be damaging. Always try to talk to you parents together. And do not allow yourself to be drawn into a situation where you may be siding with one or the other.

If your parents will not listen, it is important that you seek out help for yourself. Frankly, even if your parents are not arguing or bitter, divorce is upsetting. You should find someone to talk to, someone who is not involved. A good place to start is by making an appointment with your school counsellor. He or she can refer you to someone specific. Many Family Service Associations offer counselling to young people and in many communities and schools there are special youth clinics. Some schools and community associations also have seminars for young people whose parents are getting a separation or divorce. In these seminars, you will find other young people who are going through the same kind of situation as you.

The next question is: *What will happen when my parents get divorced?* The answer to this question depends on your parents' attitude toward and whether or not they have opted for divorce mediation, on the legal system where you live, and on the community services available.

If your parents agree to try divorce mediation first, the mediator will also talk to you. He or she will likely talk to you alone as well as with your parents. You will be able to express your feelings openly because the mediator is not "on the side" of either of your parents.

Perhaps you will live with one parent all the time, perhaps you will live with one parent and then the other, or perhaps you will visit one parent and live with the other. Discuss your feelings openly with both of your parents. Whatever the arrangement, you should be determined to keep your relationship with both your parents as natural and as close as possible. They may not want to see each other, but they will want to see and be with you. As time passes it will get easier. Most young people fear the change more than they react to the reality, which when it comes, is often a relief.

The young person whose story follows shares her feelings and experiences. Perhaps they are similar to your own. Her comments are unedited and appear just as she wrote them down for me. Her parents have been separated for two years:

> Today, I'm seventeen years old and live with my mother and younger sister. My parents both began to argue with each other about two years before they separated. Then, I was twelve and my sister was eight. I remember one night as being particularly terrible. I remember it because that was the night separation was first mentioned for real. My sister and I were downstairs in the family room building tents out of sleeping bags. Then my sister and I heard Mom and Dad upstairs. My sister went upstairs to listen. She came back crying and said that Mommy was leaving. We both started to cry and we were both scared. When our parents found out we had heard everything they both cried too. Mommy said she wasn't leaving us and promised she wouldn't go anywhere without us. We were both really upset because we were afraid we would wake up one morning and find one of our parents gone. The thought of moving was also scary. We liked the house, our schools and our friends. Since things were such a mess at home, familiar circumstances and staying in one place became really important to both of us.
>
> I remember that one of my first reactions was resentment. I knew both my parents were

involved with other people and with their own careers. I knew they had grown far apart, but I wondered, *How can they do this to me?* In some ways, though, I was better off than my sister. She was more afraid than resentful.

My parents started going to a marriage counselor. They didn't fight as much, but they didn't talk to each other much either. Then I went to the marriage counsellor, too. I don't think she helped me much because she didn't understand me. She asked who I wanted to live with and took notes.

Finally, after a long time, my dad decided to move out of the house. I remember that I wasn't worried about my life without my dad as much as I was worried about what the neighbors would think and say. I also remember feeling guilty. As though there was something I should have done, but didn't.

My father moved into an apartment a few blocks away. As soon as he was gone, he and Mother began to get on much better. He moved out in November and that first Christmas he was gone was really strange, mostly because things seemed so different.

Gradually, things really improved. It is understood that my sister and I can go to my father's whenever we want and that my dad can come here whenever he wants. We don't go there often because there isn't anything to do, but he comes here at least once a week for dinner or sometimes twice a week. Sometimes he takes us all out and sometimes he takes only my sister and me out. In the summer we go on holiday with my dad (sometimes to Europe to visit my grandparents) for two or three weeks or a month. When my mother goes on vacation Dad comes and lives in the house with us. If we are going someplace with our own friends and my dad is here, we just go ahead and leave. That way our relationship with our dad is natural. My sister is the same and not scared anymore.

Sometimes I miss my dad because he is not around all the time, but I don't miss the hostility that so often made me cry. I have thought about it a lot and I realize that my parents are very different people. They have really worked hard at trying to get along so we wouldn't be hurt anymore and both of them try to talk to us and to listen. In some ways my sister and I have the best of both worlds. I have friends whose parents are still married, but who don't get along with their parents. I also have friends whose parents are divorced and don't speak to each other. My sister and I went through a bad period, but now our parents talk to each other like friends and we have a good relationship with both of them. It's more important to have a good relationship with your parents than it is to have your parents living in one house together. We feel very lucky because our parents get on better now and their separation has not turned out to be as bad as we imagined it would be.

Not all young people feel as this girl did, but the lesson to take from her letter is that **time does help**.

CHILDREN COME FIRST

PARENTS ARE FOREVER

The following advice comes from a pamphlet called *Parents Are Forever*. It should help you and your children to cope with some of the difficult transitions you will experience in moving from the more traditional family unit to a new family structure:

Dear Parent,

As you know, a divorce or separation decree cannot and does not end your responsibility as a parent. PARENTS ARE FOREVER. Both parents should make every attempt to continue to play a vital part in the lives of their children. Children need the ongoing interest and concern of their parents. Children must feel they have two parents who love them, even though those parents could not live happily with each other.

It is our hope that the information in this pamphlet will assist you in helping your children cope with your divorce or separation with a minimum of hurt. The practical guidelines which follow are based on the many years of experience of court marriage and family counsellors.

If you are like most people, you probably have some feelings of isolation, despair, depression, loneliness, grief, guilt, and a loss of self-confidence. You are worried about many things, such as finances, a new social life, employment, fulfillment of sexual needs, and the welfare of your children. You can use this present time of difficulty as an opportunity for growth, or surrender to self-pity.

The way you cope with your divorce will in large part determine how your children cope with it. The way you feel about yourself will affect the way your children feel about themselves. Yes, you are at crossroads and can choose from alternative routes.

One road leads to self-pity, living in the past, nurturing bitterness, and turning the children against your former marriage partner. This is a dead-end road which spells trouble for you and your children.

The other road, and the constructive one, leads to becoming involved with experiences that provide opportunities for you to again feel success, to get to know yourself better, restore your self-confidence, reach out for goals that will make your life productive, satisfying, and meaningful.

The task of all parents, whether or not a marriage continues, is not easy. All parents make mistakes. But if you have a good relationship with your children and they feel your love and acceptance, they will soon forget your mistakes and remember only your goodness.[16]

4

How the Mediation Process Works

The welfare of the children remains the central focus of all discussion and/or agreements.

As a consumer of family mediation, you need to be aware of the process and procedures of mediation, as well as the role of your mediator in order for you to work together effectively. This chapter focuses on what you can expect from the divorce mediation process.

There are two types of mediation that are utilized by most family mediators. The most popular model is called **facilitative mediation**. Basically, facilitative mediation relies heavily on the ability of both parents to arrive at decisions that will be in the best interest of their children. This method will give you the best chance to be involved whereby self-determination is the key component. There will be both individual and joint sessions. You will not receive any legal advice and your mediator will control the process of the sessions, but you and your partner will be in control of the outcome and which resolutions are made.

The other approach is called **evaluative mediation**. This is where your mediator will do some advising, nudging, and directing you to arrive at a settlement that he or she feels may be in the best interest of your children. Basically, your mediator will be taking a more authoritative approach rather than a self-determining one.

In summary, facilitative mediation has a greater emphasis on self-determination, empowerment, and neutrality and it is typical of situations where there is less conflict between the parties. The evaluative mediation relies less on an emphasis of self-determination and neutrality, but with a greater need to rely on therapeutic techniques that the mediator feels will benefit the family. Typically, in an evaluative situation there is higher conflict between the parties.

Your mediator will give you advice on certain issues, spelling out the advantages and disadvantages but being very careful not to take sides with individual family members. He or she will suggest new options with regard to problems so that family members may make a more realistic decision. This means that the resolution of the dispute is based on the interpersonal process between and among family members. The decisions made are those of the family.

As already noted, I recommend that each parent has separate legal representation as they proceed through the mediation process. Often I refer them to family lawyers. The lawyers may become part of the mediation team and, if indicated, are welcome to attend mediation sessions.

The following flow chart gives you an idea of the mediation/litigation process.

The following are just some aspects of mediation that you should be aware of, and always know that you can discuss any issues regarding the process with your mediator.

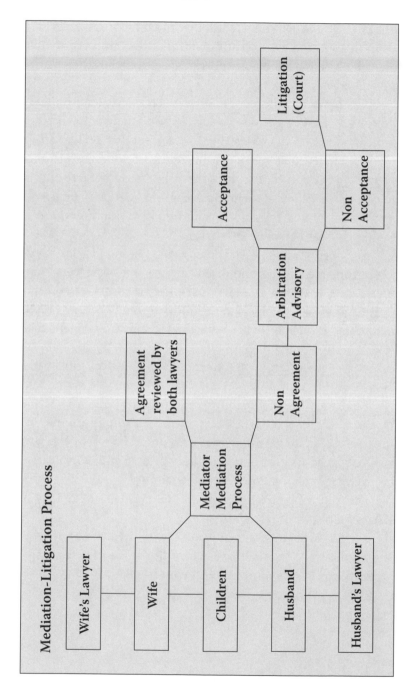

Mediation-Litigation Process

What a Mediator Does

- Schedules the mediation.
- Sets up terms, conditions, procedures.
- Explains the process.
- Establishes the ground rules.
- Helps identify and prioritize the issues.
- Gets the facts around each issue.
- Uncovers interests.
- Maintains rational, orderly discussion.
- Calls breaks, time-outs as needed.
- Suggests methods, procedures for problem-solving, when parties reach impasses.
- Balances power between parties to ensure fair procedure and balanced negotiations.
- Promotes clear, accurate communication.
- Reframes issues and inflammatory statements to reduce conflict levels.
- Makes explicit differences in assumptions, perceptions, and expectations (i.e. cultural issues).
- Picks up non-verbal communications and behaviours.

THE OVERRIDING ROLE THAT YOUR MEDIATOR PLAYS

Divorce mediation is a process of rational discussion between conflicting spouses. Your mediator acts as a neutral third party, one who has the freely given power to assist in resolution. *The interests of the children are paramount to your mediator.* In all cases, the role of your mediator is to direct discussion into productive channels, to encourage compromise, to take the attitude of problem-solving, and to prevent the type of name-calling and recrimination so prevalent in the courtroom, and in adversarial situations.

The most important goals of divorce mediation are to help you and your family arrive at an amicable settlement, to ensure that the children's interests come first, and to help you and your children understand that divorced couples are still mothers and fathers. Even if a couple has privately resolved all relevant issues related to their children, there is still good reason to enter into a mediation procedure. Your mediator has an independent goal apart from the narrowly defined interests of you and your partner, in that his or her overriding responsibility is to ensure the welfare of your children: *the welfare of the children remains the central focus of all discussion and/or agreements, no matter what the specific topic.*

Your mediator's role is advisory, but he or she also serves as a catalyst, one who encourages spouses to identify areas of disagreement directly related to separation and the settlement of their own disputes. The basis of mediation is personal responsibility and interpersonal recognition, if not respect.

Mediation practitioners have developed a variety of models in an effort to achieve these goals. Therapeutic Family Mediation stands out by its emphasis on relationships and by uncovering the emotions that may be creating conflict.

MEDIATION AND CONFLICT — THERAPEUTIC FAMILY MEDIATION

Although all spouses can give a variety of reasons for their decision to separate, beneath this rhetoric is an abiding sense of deep dissatisfaction with the relationship that is no longer tolerable for one or both of them. Such dissatisfaction speaks to conflictual patterns of relating between them that have been in place for some time and that they have been unable to change. Mutual blame for this state of affairs is commonplace and almost always associated with feelings of guilt and enmity.

Even so, many couples separate with some ambivalence, in remembrance of positive experiences in the past. Such ambivalence is quickly burned away in involvement with the adversary system, which may encourage parties to take inflexible positions in their effort to "win" against the other. In short, the dysfunctional conduct that characterizes partners in conflict does not cease on separation but rather carries on long afterward. Indeed, unless such conduct and the feelings associated with it are addressed in some way, these partners may be locked in combat long after their divorce has been ratified. Such combat, moreover, undermines their personal growth and development and may stultify their relations with all others in their life, including their children and any future relationships.

All of this is central to therapeutic family mediation. Spouses bring their various forms of dysfunction with them. It drives their conflict, affects their ability to negotiate, and predicts the likelihood that they will reach agreement. The task of a mediator, then, is to address couples' dysfunction in such a way as to allow them to take full advantage of the opportunity provided by mediation. Accordingly, to the standard goals listed above, the Therapeutic Family Mediation model superimposes several additional goals:

- To understand the subtext to couples' unresolved conflict.
- To help couples make the transition from marital roles and relations to parental roles and relations.
- To block or change patterns of conduct that are likely to interfere with productive negotiation in mediation.

- To encourage the parties to resolve any feelings of enmity toward their former partner.
- To reframe divorce in positive terms, that is, as a form of family reorganization that affords members an opportunity for a new beginning and for personal and/or family transformation.

A WORD ABOUT CO-MEDIATION

It would be worth your while to consider co-mediation, in which you work with not one mediator, but two. Usually one is male and one is female, often with different backgrounds, such as social work or law. Co-mediation has several benefits. It

- creates balance within the mediation session (i.e., male/female, social worker/attorney);
- makes it possible for one mediator to share something the other might have missed;
- provides an example of healthy, fruitful interaction that benefits your children; and
- increases efficiency of your mediation, because two practitioners can divide up their tasks.

THE MEDIATION CONTRACT

The following is a sample of a mediation contract that serves to define roles and responsibilities and protect both you and your mediator. This contract is typically drawn up after the initial phase of the mediation process.

THIS IS AN AGREEMENT BETWEEN:

Mary Johnstone

Frank Johnstone

and Howard Irving, Family Mediator

1. AGREEMENT TO MEDIATE
   The parties will participate voluntarily in mediation in an effort to resolve their differences arising from a domestic matter. This agreement sets out the terms and conditions under which the mediation will proceed. Either party or the mediator for any reason may terminate or suspend the mediation process at any time.

2. ISSUES
   The parties have agreed to mediate the following issues:

   a) care, control, and parenting of the children;
   b) spousal support;
   c) child support;
   d) possession, ownership, and division of their property; and
   e) such other issues as are made known by the parties during mediation.

3. IMPARTIALITY AND NEUTRALITY
   OF THE MEDIATOR
   The parties acknowledge that the mediator is a

professional who will assist them to communicate and will not make legal recommendations or give legal advice. The parties acknowledge that the mediator has had no previous or personal relationship with either party and that the mediator has no personal interest in the outcome of the mediation.

4. INDEPENDENT LEGAL ADVICE

The parties acknowledge that they have been advised to retain independent legal advice regarding their rights and obligations under the law and, by not doing so, risk making decisions without being fully aware of legal rights and obligations, as well as not having full knowledge of the possible legal implications and ramifications of their decisions. The parties acknowledge that the mediator will not prepare a final and binding agreement for them and that if they wish to have a mediated understanding made legally binding on each other, they will need their lawyer's assistance for that purpose. The parties agree not to make any unilateral changes to ownership or possession of property or to the status quo in relation to the child or children while mediation is in progress, unless ordered by the court or by mutual consent.

5. DISCLOSURE

The parties agree to provide each other and the mediator full disclosure of all relevant information and the required documents to ensure success of the mediation process.

6. CONFIDENTIALITY

The parties agree that any communication in the mediation process, written or verbal, will not be voluntarily disclosed to anyone who is not a party to the mediation. The only situations where there would be exceptions to this understanding are as follows:

a) complying with any obligations imposed by law (e.g., child or elder abuse);

b) protecting the lives, safety, and well-being of any persons;

The parties agree that anything said or an admission or communication made while participating in the mediation process cannot be used in current or subsequent court proceedings. The parties acknowledge that the mediator may request to meet privately with each party during the mediation or request to see the child or children or other interested parties, and the mediator will only inform the other party of such information where, in the sole discretion of the mediator, such information is relevant to the issues in dispute and the disclosure would assist in the resolution of the issues.

The parties agree that they will not call the mediator as a witness in any legal proceeding to their opinions or to disclose any admission or communication made to him or her in the course of mediation. If, however, the mediator is subpoenaed, then the client is responsible for all legal costs and the mediator's fees and expenses.

7. USER FEES

Private Service: We agree to share equally or proportionately (husband percentage, wife percentage), or _____ alone agrees to pay the fees and disbursements for the mediation services provided, for preparation of any documents or reports, including but not limited to time for interviews; reading reports and documentation; telephone conversations with the clients, lawyers, or other collateral sources; preparing correspondence; and other relevant activities. Disbursements and other out-of-pocket expenses incurred by the mediator, such as photocopying, long-distance telephone calls, facsimile transmissions, and messenger services, will be billed additionally. Travel time (if any) will be billed at half the normal rate.

We agree to pay an hourly rate of $___ per hour, subject to change upon notice by the mediator. We also understand that we will be billed for appointments that are cancelled if there is less than 24 (twenty-four) hours' notice prior to cancellation.

We agree to pay this rate at the end of each and every mediation session.

8. CONSULTATION, INTERNS, AND OBSERVERS

The parties understand and agree that the mediator may have a co-mediator in the mediation process. The participation of co-mediators in the mediation process will be subject to the same duty of confidentiality as the mediator.

Parent No. 1 Signature _____

Parent No. 2 Signature _____

Mediator's Signature _____

THE THREE PHASES OF MEDIATION

Phase 1: Exploration and Assessment

The first discussions are usually carried out between your mediator and each individual family member. It is critical for the mediator to thoroughly explain the mediation process at this time. *About 10 percent of couples coming to mediation end up deciding to reconcile. This is why good mediators always explore the possibility of reconciliation.* This is a period of individual introspection and the mediator simply tries to understand where each individual stands as well as what each wants to accomplish. The mediator will listen to what is said, but will also observe what is done.

Your mediator's ability to empathize is critical to this phase. He or she must be able to accept, understand, and support the family member so that real expression can take place. The focus is not only on how the individual feels about a specific problem at hand, but also on self-perception. This process creates an atmosphere of trust between client and mediator. The major intent is to identify and clarify problems, while offering constant emotional support. Each relevant family member is approached in the same way, given an opportunity to ventilate the anger and hurt according to each person's unique situation, while being able to explore and focus on his or her unique problems.

When you first meet your mediator he or she will probably review certain steps that both you and your partner will follow.

Your mediator will

- affirm your willingness to seek a co-operative solution to your problems.
- describe the litigation option.
- contrast the litigation option with the mediation option.
- define family mediation and the mediator's roles.
- indicate that the mediator is committed to being impartial.
- emphasize that the mediator's bias is to favour the children's best interests.
- describe mediation procedures.
- define the limits of confidentiality.
- describe the fee rate, payment method, and mediation contract.
- answer any questions you may have.
- affirm a joint commitment to begin the mediation process.

While assessment is an ongoing activity throughout the mediation process, it is most concentrated in this initial phase, with two immediate concerns in mind.

The first concern is whether you should move on to Phase 2 (negotiation), or to Phase 3 (resolution). The decision depends on whether there are issues present that would likely produce an impasse. Such issues include relational dysfunction (such as a high level of controlled conflict), poor affective control (either generally or with regard to specific emotionally charged issues), or rigid positions. In such cases, you would enter Phase 2. In their absence, you would move on to Phase 3.

Specific questions should cover physical, emotional, and economic violence. The following are questions recommended by the National Committee on Violence Against Women:

1. Has your partner ever hit, punched, slapped, kicked, bitten you, pulled your hair, or pushed you around?
2. Has your partner ever forced you to engage in sexual acts against your will?
3. Has your partner ever destroyed or damaged any of your belongings or property or hurt any of your pets?
4. Have you ever applied to a court for a protection order?
5. Does your partner ever try to convince you that you are mentally ill?[17]

If the responses to these questions identify abuse, referrals should be made to agencies or organizations that ensure the safety of women and children. Your case should not be accepted for mediation.

Your mediator will facilitate the sessions. This includes

- explaining rules and procedures;
- choosing who has the floor;
- listing standards of practice;
- helping couples tone down disruptive behaviour;
- defining and selecting issues for discussion;
- determining with the couple which meetings are with them separately and which together;
- maintaining a safe environment;
- handling termination sessions/service; and
- referring aspects of the case to an appropriate service.

The following are questions your mediator will ask to determine whether you are amenable to mediation:

- Do you have a clear understanding of the mediation process?
- Can you articulate specific proposals regarding these issues?
- Are you capable of separating marital from parental issues?
- Can you control your feelings?
- How well or poorly do you communicate with each other?
- Can you distinguish between your self-interest and the best interests of the children?
- Can you together negotiate issues to closure?
- Can you together focus on one issue at a time?
- Can you together stay in the present (without repeatedly trying to fight old marital battles)?
- Can you together begin to consider what sort of future you want to create for your family?

If the answer to these and related questions is a clear or at least substantial yes, then you are probably a good candidate for family mediation and a mediation agreement will be drawn up and signed. (See sample agreement, page 87.) I say "probably" because the assessment process is ongoing. The initial evidence of amenability may later prove incorrect as you address specific issues.

Conversely, if the answer to these questions is a clear or at least substantial no, then you are a poor candidate for mediation at this time. You may be referred on for short-term therapy, after which you may wish to return to mediation for another assessment. If this therapy is unproductive, you may be referred on to litigation. On average, 80 to 90 percent of the clients we see in private mediation are found amenable for family mediation.

When working with families, mediators consider communication as the *sine qua non* of family operations. All communication, verbal or non-verbal, in some ways describes the nature of the relationship between and among the members of the family; accordingly, all behaviour has interactional significance and can be thought of as synonymous with communication. This has become apparent from what has become a well-known principle that "one cannot *not* communicate." The husband or wife who comes home from work and says nothing to his or her partner and children while walking past them in the family room is really communicating something.

The above is a good example of putting communication into context. Every piece of communication has to be considered in terms of what is happening to the people who are communicating. Someone once asked George Bernard Shaw, the famous playwright, what one book he would read if ever he were marooned on an island in the South Pacific. His quick response was *"How to Get Off an Island When You Are Marooned in the South Pacific."*

Your mediator is always on the lookout to help family members clarify indirect and distorted messages. He does this primarily by engaging the family members themselves in talking to each other. He will observe how the family or couple interact so that he or she can understand how the family operates. Your mediator will also pay close attention to ways messages are sent and received as well as the degree of clarity and directness of communication. He will try to reduce the destructive conflict and set a framework for non-accusatory blaming from one member to the other. He will try to clarify faulty communication by giving the family members an opportunity to make some of the implicit communication explicit.

It is only with understanding that you and your family can move on to dispute resolution. The mediator engages the family members by asking direct questions and framing the questions so that members in the interview relate to each other and to the mediator. An example might be, "You seem puzzled at what she just said, so why don't you ask her to explain more clearly what she means?"

Phase 2: Negotiation

This is the critical negotiation phase that eventually leads to the resolution of disputes. During this phase it is extremely important that family members interact with one another. The focus shifts from the mediator to the family — joint interviews are held with the couple, or may include the entire family if the situation demands collective consultation. Each person explains his or her goals and expresses what is really wanted.

The individual positions discovered in Phase 1 are discussed among the parties involved. These views are discussed in two ways: (1) as stated by the individual spouse; and (2) as they are understood by other family members.

This latter point is extremely important and warrants further explanation. The American writer Oliver Wendell Holmes once wrote a short piece entitled "The Three Johns" as part of his larger work, *The Autocrat at the Breakfast Table*.[18] Its theme was that "John" was not one person, but three persons. He was

1. John, as he perceived himself;
2. John, as perceived by his conversational partner; and
3. John, as he actually is.

The idea was simple: for every two people in a conversation there are, in reality, six. Holmes goes on to illustrate the real difficulties of communication between the two individuals who are really six.

As the old saying goes, "Never mind what I say, listen to what I mean." This is, more often than not, the task of the mediator. A wife might say to her estranged husband, "You can see the children whenever you want. Just call before you come." The wife is asking her estranged partner to respect her privacy, but what does "call before you come" really mean? The husband may well interpret this to mean he should call twenty minutes before arriving, when, in fact, the wife meant she wanted two days' warning.

This is an oversimplified example of misunderstanding in communication, but it illustrates the role of your mediator. He must be certain that people express their real desires and goals and, equally important, that the other party understands. By clearing up family miscommunication, your mediator assists in clarifying ambiguous issues. Your mediator helps the family members go beyond the initial presentation of the issue, so that they may have a firmer grasp of the real problem.

When there is an impasse, your mediator will attempt to reframe the conflict by broadening perspectives and offering you options not previously realized; for example, in a situation where the parents are in disagreement as to the amount of time the children should spend with each of them, they may be so concerned with their own objectives that they have not considered what would be best for the children. The mediator can help the parents see how they must set aside their own personal interests when those interests conflict with those of the children. This is usually achieved during discussions that include both the children and the parents.

Your mediator should use the following techniques to help you resolve the issues you are facing:

- Identify what each spouse perceives as the issue(s).
- Discover the position of each spouse on each issue, giving the spouses an opportunity to give their individual opinions.
- Investigate the extent to which each spouse's position and individual interests coincide.

- Establish the extent to which both spouses think it possible to achieve a fair and equitable agreement.
- Assist the couple in setting out the terms and conditions of an informal agreement.

The next step is a discussion that will hopefully lead to final resolution of the issues. This includes:

- Exploring the consequences of alternatives.
- Breaking (or "fractionating") large issues into smaller ones, those that open up room to manoeuvre.
- Keeping the conflict fluid by focusing on several issues rather than on the one on which the spouses appear to be stuck.
- Exploring "what if" scenarios.
- Having brief "time outs" to give the spouses the chance to get control of their feelings.
- Broadening the alternatives available to the couple by citing options that have worked for other couples.

For a more fully comprehensive treatment of family mediation, see *Therapeutic Family Mediation* by Irving and Benjamin.[19]

Phase Three: Resolution

This phase of divorce mediation usually takes a highly structured form. It is almost contractual in nature and details what each party will do.

Each step is monitored so that everyone concerned knows what action is being taken on any agreement made. If either party does not act as agreed upon, there will be almost immediate feedback. This reduces the "revolving door syndrome" of going back to the courts.

In many cases the emotional entanglement during and after separation may lead to a great deal of resentment on the part of one individual in the family. Before proper mediation can be effective, this individual may need to take advantage of more intensive psychological therapy outside the mediation process. This type of therapy is called *crisis intervention* and it is normally a short-term process. It may be undertaken simultaneously with the divorce mediation process.

It is important to understand that your mediator will be taking a "systems" approach to the family. That is, he or she will assume that if one member is affected, the entire family "system" is also affected. This is why it is crucial for the mediator to be able to see all family members who may be involved. The best way to describe the role of the mediator would be to define him or her as a "facilitator." The mediator's main objective is the resolution of family disputes in the context of what is best for the children.

To sum up, your mediator will: provide emotional support; help identify the problem(s); elicit sufficient factual information to find a solution to the problem(s); develop and identify all possible alternative solutions; evaluate the probable outcome of alternative solutions; assist the couple to mutually select one of the alternatives; develop an agreement covering the steps that must be taken in order for the selected alternative to be successful; and follow up or monitor the success of such an agreement.

Be forewarned that your lawyer and/or your partner's lawyer may become uneasy when confronted with the divorce mediation process. Some lawyers instruct their clients not to reveal certain information for fear that it will be held against them in a subsequent court case. It is therefore very important, if you have already engaged a lawyer by this point, that the lawyer understands the mediation process, and that they be reassured that information discussed is considered privileged.

To ensure the highest degree of co-operation, I always have the lawyers and my clients sign an agreement that includes a clause stating that "Evidence of anything said or of any admission or communication made in the course of mediation is not admissible in the pending or any other legal proceedings. The mediator may not be called as a witness or on behalf of either parent (party) in the pending or any other legal proceeding, and the mediator shall not be required or permitted in the pending or any other legal proceeding to give opinion or to disclose any admission or communication made to him in the course of mediation."

The following is an example of an agreement regarding the mediation process:

Mediation:
A report will indicate the number of interviews, the persons who attended the interviews, and the terms of any agreement reached. It will also indicate any issues upon which agreement was not reached. Otherwise, evidence of anything, said or done or if any admission or communication made in the course of mediation is not admissible in any ongoing or future Court proceedings relevant to the issues in mediation.

Dated the _____ of _____ 20__, in the City of _____,_____

Name: _____   /

Name of Witness:_____

Signature: _____

Signature of Witness:_____

WHAT HAPPENS NEXT?

Once you have gone through the three phases of mediation, you are ready to discuss your parenting agreement. If agreement is reached, the details are written down and referred back to your respective lawyers. The lawyers will then read and discuss the agreement with you before signing. The agreement is a result of mutual co-operative problem-solving. The following two chapters deal with creating a shared-parenting plan.

5

Shared Parenting: What Is It and Can You Make It Work?

Shared parenting is not for everyone, and its benefits are available only to those families who are willing to make a considerable effort.

One weekend afternoon, go to any zoo, park or movie theatre in your area and you'll find them easily: the single "Disneyland parents," trying desperately to amuse and care for their children during the few short hours that custody decisions allow them. Drive through your neighbourhood in winter and you'll see the children, bundled to the eyes, grasping a toy, standing on the stoop, waiting for a father that can't come in. How painful for both parents and child when that inevitable moment comes: "be a good kid, I'll see you next week; remember I love you."

But **it doesn't have to be this way.** The goal in this chapter is to help you avoid being a Disneyland parent as described above.

What is shared parenting? In shared parenting, both of you share the parental responsibilities and rights regarding the children. Shared parenthood does not mean a rigid formula of equality between the parents. It means that both contribute what they can in a way that is most beneficial to the children and to their own needs and rights as parents. **Shared parenting maintains the parental bond even though the marital bond has ended.**

Shared parenting is a relatively new phenomenon that reflects changes in the structure and thinking of society. Today, traditional parental roles are changing rapidly. Women are firmly ensconced in the work force, while many men have taken an increasingly active role in parenting their children. What this means for divorced couples is that traditional custody arrangements are neither adequate nor beneficial for children or parents. For these reasons, the idea of shared parenting has emerged as a positive step that may alleviate some of the painful problems. Proper circumstances are necessary, though, and in my experience the availability of a trained mediator is extremely important to success.

But the big shift in thinking has happened, and is still happening, in the philosophy of family law itself, and that is what is now trickling down into the public perception of parenting after divorce.

Historically, family law statutes have been centred on a concern with the individual rights of adult parents; children, if they were seen at all, were treated as chattel. Thus, the language of the law and inevitably of its practitioners was the language of ownership and possession. Concerns about "winning" or "losing" custody had and have little to do with children and much to do with an adult struggle over power and control over property. However, during the past fifteen years or so, such language has become obsolete. This is the case for several reasons:

- An increasing awareness of the reciprocal character of relations between parents and children.
- A recognition of the important role fathers play in the development of their children, both male and female.

- An increasing sensitivity to issues of equality, one of the many consequences of the contemporary feminist movement.
- The extraordinary influx of women into the workforce, with consequences in the organization of family systems.
- The rapid and sustained rise in the proportion of families with "joint" or "shared" parenting arrangements.
- Recognition of the negative impact on children of ongoing parental conflict, including litigation over control of the children and subsequent variations.

The upshot of these various reasons has been statutory changes, or recommendations for change, that emphasize the central importance of parenting plans and the associated shift in language from child custody to shared responsibility and the preferred use of family mediation.

TWO RESPONSES TO SHARED PARENTING

There are two typical responses to the idea of shared parenting. The first but less common reaction is intense excitement over a new and possibly workable solution to a thorny issue. If the concept is accepted as a serious effort to provide the emotional stability that children need without cutting off one parent, then it can be highly creative and innovative. It should not, however, merely be seen as "trendy."

The second and far more prevalent attitude begins with a horrified expression and ends with a statement like, "That's impossible — how could parents tear their children apart like that?"

It's true that every child has an emotional bond with both parents that should not be arbitrarily broken. However, is it really better in every case for one parent to move out and become merely a special visitor on specified weekends? Or can divorced couples, believing that parents really are forever, eliminate emotional and financial inequality by totally sharing the responsibilities of parenting?

I pose these questions frankly, because the children of divorce have sat in my office crying for their parents to stop fighting, hoping they will not have to lose their mother or father. My office has even served as a child drop-off zone during custody battles when one spouse does not want the other to know a home address.

More and more parents are finding that the idea of shared parenting is not only possible but beneficial for the entire family. Shared parenting is hard work for everyone. It is difficult to establish and maintain, but it is an extremely positive way to ensure that children are not traumatized by losing one parent. Parents do not have to assume an unnatural role, and children are less likely to be put in a position where they are playing one parent off against the other.

Ideally, a shared-parenting plan is the natural outflow of divorce mediation. This part of mediation begins with an exploration with the parents of the feasibility of shared parenting in their case. If it does seem worthwhile in a particular case, then the mediator will assist in setting out the details and regulations.

CLEARING THE GROUND FOR SHARED PARENTING

Many preconceptions and difficulties need to be cleared up before shared parenting can become a functioning process. The initial fear that children may be torn apart between two separate homes must be balanced against the trauma involved in an artificial visiting-parent situation. The idea that the different lifestyles of divorced parents might result in conflict and disorientation has to be faced. What if the rag doll or the bicycle is at one home and not at the other? What about the conflicting loyalties that may arise due to the different regulations enforced in different households? Can children cope with the varying expectations of their parents any more than they could within the nuclear family?

After assisting in setting up many shared-parenting arrangements, I can say that children are far more adaptable than adults may believe. School-age children, especially, have to enter an alien environment every day — an environment that has different surroundings, demands, and rules than their own homes — and most do so without undue stress.

Most children can adapt quickly to a shared-parenting arrangement as long as they are aware of its shape and as long as it is consistently supported by each parent. Instead of being torn apart by such a situation, they generally feel more secure than they would under other conditions. It gives kids a sense of security to know that although their parents no longer live together, each one is actively participating in their lives.

SHARED PARENTING IS NOT A SILVER BULLET

Shared parenting is not for everyone, and its benefits are available only to those families who are willing to make a considerable effort. When it works, shared parenting does not require a child to make a stated or implied choice between mother and father. It creates a situation instead where both parents are kept, where the tale-telling and present-buying inherent in Sunday parenting are not nearly so prevalent, and where each parent is able to re-establish a viable personal life during the times when the children are living in the other household. The prerequisites are adaptability and understanding on the children's part, commitment and respect for viewpoints on the parents' part.

Adaptability is to be highly valued in the process of putting a parenting plan into practice. The design of a house may look wonderful on paper but prove to be impractical once it's lived in for a while. Similarly, some parenting plans may look good on paper but not work with regard to certain details, especially in how your children experience it in action. Parents need to review their plans in light of such experiences and be open to mutually agreeable revisions.

A shared arrangement can improve or deteriorate for a number of reasons, including a child's maturing understanding of his or her parents, remarriages, or altered living conditions. Your mediator's primary responsibilities to you in this light are threefold. He or she

- must be able to find out whether it is acceptable to parents and children alike as the best method of caring for the children;
- should assist in setting up reasonable and fair living arrangements; and
- must be available as an adviser as the arrangement continues.

Shared parenting is not a panacea for all the damage done to children by divorce, nor does it obliterate the fact that many divorced parents frankly dislike each other. Under the proper circumstances, however, your mediator can act as a buffer between the parents. One of the major principles of mediation of any kind is to keep the welfare of the children foremost. Your mediator's role in shared parenting is no different.

One important caution for anyone considering the idea of shared parenting: this approach usually requires more contact and co-operation between the spouses and should not be entered into as a means of maintaining distance from wife to husband or husband to wife. This approach to shared parenting is no better than a custody battle. It usually does not work and often undermines the entire situation. A firm commitment from both of you is necessary; mere acquiescence on the part of one spouse will not do.

The following is what I call "How to fail at shared parenting:"

1. Parents agree between themselves through a shared-parenting arrangement because one parent's chief motivation is that this will lead to reconciliation.
2. Parents agree to shared parenting because one parent feels intimidated and is fearful that financial support will be cut off.
3. Parents agree to shared parenting because one parent feels guilty at ending the marriage and wants to make it up to the other parent.
4. Parents agree to shared parenting because they are pressured by therapists, marriage counsellors, mediators, parents, and friends.

Some time ago, I conducted some empirical research regarding shared parenting. My feeling at that time was that we had no evidence as to whether or not shared parenting was an effective model of parenting after divorce. The study was conducted with 201 shared-parenting families and 194 sole-custody parents. Those who were the most successful were found in the shared-parenting sample. They had low to moderate levels of separation conflict; they maintained a child-centred orientation to parenting, and showed motivation by both parents to accept and overcome complications and challenges that arose. There was a much higher level of satisfaction for those parents involved in shared parenting than there was for those with sole custody. We also found that there was a much higher level of compliance with financial obligations with shared parenting than with sole custody.[20]

The rest of this chapter is devoted to three actual cases that I conducted in my practice. They are transcribed from a video recording. The names have been changed and some of the content has been altered to maintain confidentiality.

CASE 1: JOANNE AND PETER HENDERSON

A positive and common picture of shared parenting may be seen in the case of the Henderson family.

Background

Peter and Joanne Henderson had one son, Mike, now eleven, and one daughter, Kate, now ten. The Hendersons were legally divorced. During their separation, both children lived with their mother and the father was allowed generous access.

As time progressed, it became apparent that Kate preferred to live with her mother, while Mike was closer to his father. This was not the result of jockeying on the part of either spouse but simply of emotional attachments that seem fairly predictable in such a family.

Joanne suggested that they split the children between them to allow for their preferences, but Peter did not want to lose either of his children, even though he might be gaining one.

Through conversations with his friends and as a result of reading, Peter became aware of shared parenting. He didn't know how to set this arrangement up himself or how to broach it with Joanne, with whom he did not communicate well. Eventually a mutual friend put him in touch with me.

After I met with Peter and Joanne, I could see that this couple was not at all interested in reconciliation, yet each one was very much involved in the welfare of their children.

A series of brief interviews resulted in setting up a shared-parenting agreement. It stipulated that both children would live with each parent during alternate weeks. Joanne and Peter arranged to live within three blocks of each other so the kids would not have to adapt to new schools and neighbourhoods. This situation has been working well now for eight months.

The Interview

Peter: I really can't believe that this is working so well. Joanne's been just great about it. We worked out the details at her house. The kids knew that it was my idea and I think they were afraid this might cause problems. But it was Joanne who made up the calendars with different colors representing the alternate weeks so we'd both have something to put on our fridge. The kids accepted the fact that we both wanted to do this and it quieted many of their fears about it.

Joanne: Well, we told them [the children] that we were trying something new, that we were kind of pioneers, and we'd all have to work hard to make it go well. This intrigued them and they began to get excited about it.

Peter: Of course, we were concerned about the kids getting disoriented, but since our places are so close together there really doesn't seem to be any problem. The first few times the switch was made there were a few problems about homework, but these have been cleared up. It was just that at the time there were too many things going on in their lives.

During the interview, I asked several questions involving possessions and how rules were made. Joanne told me that many of Kate's things stayed at her house, but she had quite a few at Peter's and didn't seem to mind because she always knew where they were. Many of Mike's things, his bike and so on, were usually at his father's house, but Mike, too, wasn't concerned about any inconvenience this caused him.

Peter and Joanne have conflicting philosophies of life and parenting and these are expressed to some extent in their lifestyles.

Peter: I'm not as strict about cleaning up the house, but I am adamant about homework, making time to talk, and not watching so much television. There were a few times when one of the kids would say that they were allowed to watch this program or that at their mother's, but I explained that we felt differently about these things, and that this was how it was to be here. In thinking about it now, I'm amazed that they understood this and accepted it so quickly. Regulations are very important. You have to make it clear that the time spent with you is normal time, not playtime. The kids have to realize that you have your lifestyle and it has to be respected.

Joanne: At first, I was very concerned that the kids would pick up bad habits outside. Peter's not the neatest person in the world, but it seemed to work out well once the kids understood that we lived different lives. While I'm trying to relax after a hard day, I sometimes don't have the energy to spend with them, and I admit that they were really getting hooked on television. This was mostly when I was caring for them myself, but now that they spend alternate weeks with Peter this has been cut down and I'm pleased about that.

With some time off, I find I have more time to spend with the kids when they are with me. Because we live pretty close together, possessions really aren't a problem. We don't get into duplicating things — neither of us could afford it anyway. In some ways, it's good for the kids to have to plan what to bring from one place to another.

* * *

111

I spoke to the children, Mike and Kate, to find out what they thought about the situation. They told me that they really weren't too hopeful in the beginning, but that "Mom and Dad wanted to try it." At the time we spoke, though, they had nothing negative to say about the arrangement. Kate thought her father was tough about homework, and Mike didn't like having to keep his room at his mother's so clean, but these things were said in a tone of grudging admiration more than anything else. Both agreed that they liked being able to know both their parents in this manner, rather than living with their mother and having their father visit, as in the past.

This shared-parenting approach was in some ways ideal for this situation. The calendar was quite fluid. If one spouse had a week off, then it was quite possible to rearrange schedules to suit conditions. Although Peter and Joanne did not communicate well, they were completely committed to the idea of both providing the affection their children need. In Joanne's words, "I would never give up my kids, but I can't expect Peter to either. His ideas are different than mine, but he's a good father. It wouldn't be fair to cut the kids off from that."

And Peter said, "Joanne and I don't get along, that's why we're divorced, but we can't let that get in the kids' way."

Joanne said she was finding that there were some lifestyle benefits to the situation: "When the kids were both living with me all the time, I couldn't really go out much myself. There was always the problem of babysitters and I really didn't feel I could ask Peter if I was dating somebody. There were other problems. I mean, what if I met somebody that I wanted to be with? I really couldn't stay out late or anything and it got to be quite difficult. Now, since the kids are away every other week, I can begin to have a social life and this is very good for me. I know they are getting the best care and I don't have to worry."

Peter's reaction was similar: "You know, when you're married you really don't get involved in some things with your kids. You know, little things, like doctor's visits and dentist appointments. I remember the first time we went out to buy clothes. In the past, I had never done this with the kids, and it was really an incredible [experience to] watch them picking out things they liked. The same kind of thing happened when we went out to buy food. I didn't stock the kind of stuff they like at first, and they thought it was a riot that I didn't know what Fruit Loops were."

"Socially I guess my life has changed, too; it is more restricted now than it was, but I really don't mind. I feel much easier now about my whole life, knowing that I'm participating in my kids' lives. I can't tell you how bad those Sunday visits were. I kept thinking, 'Christ, what are we going to do now?'"

As for the future, Joanne said, "Peter and I have talked about what might happen if anything more permanent comes up in either of our lives. No decisions have been made about that yet, and I think we both hope we'll be able to work it out if it does. We did tell the kids that we were kind of pioneers in this, and I guess we are, so we'll just have to overcome that obstacle when it turns up."

Reflections

To me the most encouraging thing about the Henderson family is that the children, Mike and Kate, found their lives to be quite normal. They felt secure in the knowledge that both parents actively loved them. I think that during my joint interview with them, they were beginning to wonder what was wrong with me: I was looking for reactions and problems that just weren't there.

The major reason that shared parenting is working so well for the Hendersons springs from the fact that they are both totally committed to their children. This commitment is the bottom line of shared parenting. Two other reasons that the logistics were favourable were the proximity of the couple's homes and the fact that the children themselves were able to deal with the arrangement psychologically.

ONGOING MEDIATION

What happens when conflicts arise in a shared-parenting arrangement? Ideally the mediator will be retained to mediate these situations. This stops the parents, at least initially, from involving lawyers and courts to resolve their disputes. At first, parents may get into difficulty regarding what seem to be very minor issues. For example:

- "Why is it that Sally watches television at her father's when I have made a rule that she is not allowed to watch television on a school night?"
- "When Leo returns after the week with his mother, he tells me that I don t know how to cook and that his mother gives him good meals and I give him all this junk food."

There is no doubt that shared parenting cannot fully replace a traditional family situation that has harmony, although we must admit that many intact families have severe conflicts when it comes to child-rearing practices.

CASE 2: ADELE AND GORD WATKINS — SHARED PARENTING, OR IS IT?

Background

This couple was originally referred by their lawyers for mediation over custody and access issues regarding their seven-year-old daughter, Margaret. However, this couple showed itself to be open to mediation in a broader sense.

In fact, assessment over three sessions suggested that they were ready to move immediately to negotiation and resolution. Both seemed mature, rational, and fully aware that their marriage was finished. Each respected the other's parenting ability, and each had a good relationship with Margaret.

The shared parenting concept was eagerly accepted by each spouse. An arrangement was worked out whereby Margaret would live with her mother for one week, her father for one week, with a mid-week crossover where Margaret could spend an evening with the other parent. Vacation time would be split equally with a mid-week crossover.

Margaret would attend the same school, since she was doing well there and it was roughly halfway between both parents' homes. Similarly, all child-care costs would be shared equally, because both parents had well-established careers (he as a civil engineer, she as a university professor of English literature) and earned roughly the same income.

Over the first six months, the parenting agreement functioned well. The parents talked regularly in a friendly way about Margaret's welfare and the logistics of their situation.

Then Adele met and entered into a relationship with Richard. After several months, they decided to move in together. They were willing to continue with shared parenting as Richard did not feel he had a right, or the need, to interfere with the plan.

Gord's reaction was quite different. When Adele told him that she and Richard had decided to live together in her home, he became terrified that another man would replace him as Margaret's father, and was jealous of Richard's relationship with Adele.

Because Gord's relationship with Adele had been friendly and functional around parenting issues over the past year, he fantasized from time to time about the possibility of a future reconciliation. His fears and resentments about Adele's new relationship with Richard expressed themselves in his desire to apply for sole custody of Margaret.

This shook Adele's commitment to shared parenting. Concerned that the only reason her former husband had agreed to the arrangement initially was to stay involved with her, she, too, planned to apply for sole custody.

As for Margaret, she had adjusted extremely well to the shared-parenting system. However, in the face of these recent troubles, she began having difficulty sleeping and repeatedly asked her parents why they couldn't live together again.

In an effort to resolve these difficulties, the Watkins returned to the mediation process, this time with me because their first mediator was not available.

Joint Session

Mediator: I've been doing mediation for a number of years and have a particular interest in helping people come up with co-operative parenting arrangements. I was really pleased to find out that you have been one of those groups of pioneers who went into shared parenting, and were able to make it work. I see so many terrible, conflictual situations with parents grabbing and manipulating their children. I compliment you on the fact that you have worked well together in having a good shared-parenting relationship.

Although subsequent questioning established both parents' respect for each other's parenting ability, it also revealed what was to be the first of three central stumbling blocks in the case — Gord's continued attachment to his former wife.

Gord: Well, Margaret is a lot like her mother in many ways. She's very nice, very pleasant to be with and I love her so much.

The second concerned Gord's fear that the shift in Adele's romantic situation would eventually mean loss of contact with his daughter. This fear became apparent as the mediator sought to reinterpret the issue of child custody from a marital issue to a parenting issue, with the emphasis on Margaret's likely experience.

Next, it became clear that Adele was seeking sole custody only because Gord was doing so. She would have preferred to continue their shared-parenting arrangement because it had been working well. As would Gord; it was Richard's presence, the second stumbling block, that was causing him grief.

Later, he made his fear crystal clear:

Gord: Well, in a lot of these cases, you know, I mean, when there is a step-parent that moves in, and I think you know that, and you'll agree with me, that in a lot of these cases the father's role becomes next to none.

The third stumbling block was Gord's sense of anger and betrayal that Adele hadn't discussed her relationship with Richard with him. Gord felt that he then could have been better prepared for her decision to move in with Richard.

This series of stumbling blocks was based in the past, in Gord's continuing attachment to Adele and his fantasy that one day they could reconcile. Because this line of reasoning would inevitably lead to an impasse, much of the balance of the session was directed toward repeatedly reinterpreting the issues in parental rather than marital terms. At one point, this focus was stated succinctly:

Mediator: How can the two of you continue to be good parents and give your daughter everything she deserves?

Realizing that this shift would require more work than could be accomplished in one session, I used the last few minutes to set up the next series of individual sessions, especially those with Gord. I did so in two steps. First, I reinterpreted Gord's objections in parental terms:

Mediator: I must admit, I don't know how you feel about it, Adele, but I think it does show a lot of strength on Gord's part to be as concerned as he is about his daughter. Would you agree?

Adele: Yeah, I do respect his concern for Margaret.

Second, I suggested that only more discussion would unearth the real issues underlying the current problem, including the views of the other players in this drama.

Interview — Margaret and Richard

Mediator: What I would like to do, if it makes sense, because I don't know enough about this situation, and I don't know enough about you, and I feel that even in this afternoon's session that I am feeling a little bit pulled here, is I would like to get together with you ... individually, to explore a little more. I think I could get a little closer to your real concerns if I saw you individually.

I would also like your permission to meet with Margaret because she's the one who probably has some questions. Obviously there is something going on because she's not feeling as good as she did about the situation.

I had three goals for my individual session with Gord: to get him to explicitly articulate the stumbling blocks hinted at in the first session; to reinterpret them as his problem; and to juxtapose this personal problem against his daughter's needs. The first goal was easily accomplished. Gord readily admitted to his continuing emotional investment with Adele:

Gord: I think any human being who had the kind of relationship I had with Adele doesn't stop hoping. I'd only be kidding myself.

He also readily acknowledged his anger and disappointment with Adele.

Gord: Right now, we're not able to reach agreement. I don't want to put blame, but if Richard hadn't moved in — I know, obviously, he must be important to her — but if he hadn't been in the picture, I really think we wouldn't have had these problems. I'm even prepared to say that if he hadn't come on so suddenly, if it had been more gradual, let's say if the dating had been spread over a longer period of time.... If Adele would've sat down and said, "Gord, we've got to talk. I'm concerned about the impact of this ... how we're going to approach it."

Mediator: It might have been a lot easier for you.

The second goal required an interpretation that shifted Gord's reaction to Adele's relationship as his problem, specifically one of loss and mourning.

Mediator: You know what's happening to you? What's happening to you is that there's been a sort of delay. Initially, when people are confronted with the fact that their marriage may be over they feel the pain and the emptiness and the hurt and the sorrow. And I think in the beginning, it probably didn't hit you as hard. But now I think you're going through that grieving process. You look very unhappy to me. You look sad. Are you sad?

Gord: *I am sad, yeah. I am unhappy.*

Mediator: *It's been a real loss to you.... Let's talk about the loss for you of Adele.*

Gord: *If we're talking about the loss of Adele, we're talking about the loss of my daughter, too. My daughter reminds me of her.*

Mediator: *And the house. You had to move out of that house, which I'm sure meant something to you, too.*

Gord: *That's right. We had a nice arrangement of sharing back and forth.*

Mediator: *So it's almost like your whole world is....*

The final goal proved more difficult. To get at it, I posed a question that emphasized the distinction between marital and parenting issues.

Mediator: *There are two things that you need to work out. One is how you're going through this hurtful, painful situation of disengaging from your wife. How you're going to be able to do that and be a good parent like you have been. That's the challenge. How can you do these two things?*

Initially, Gord resisted, seeing the two as tied together:

Gord: *Well, I think that sometimes you reach a point in your life when you go for broke [re: sole custody]. I think maybe I'm going for broke.*

In response, I persisted in separating the issues, implying, too, that linking them the way Gord had done had made it increasingly difficult for him to continue to be the good parent he was striving to be.

Mediator: Let's not discuss sole custody right now. Let's talk about the two things. The disengaging emotionally from Adele, that that's over, and being a good parent. How are you going to do that?

Gord: I thought I was doing that. You're saying to me I'm not. Obviously you're sensing that I'm not.

Mediator: You seem very hurt by this. I have a feeling, and I may be wrong about this, that a lot of your energy is being tied up in this sadness, and that you can't do as much as you'd like to do.

Gord: Um-hum.

Mediator: Would you like it if you had the ability, and you may not have it now, but would you like to be able to say, "I've got to be able to begin a new life, and as much as I would like it, it's not going to happen. She's not coming back. And I have got to begin a new life, for myself and for my daughter." Is that what you would like to be able to do?

Gord: Yeah.

Mediator: Okay, would you like me to help you try and do that?

Gord: How would you help me do it?

Mediator: I don't know yet. But would you like me to help you? So the two of us try....

Gord: What happens in the meantime? Life goes on.

Mediator: In the meantime, you will continue to be a good parent.

Gord: What does that mean, "continue to be a good parent"?

Mediator: And Adele is going to continue to be a good mother. Well, one thing would be to stop the lawsuit and stop fighting about who should have sole custody. That would be one thing, in my opinion. And to give as much attention as you can to your daughter without being preoccupied with Richard and Adele. Those would be two things. And there may be other things. But, you're going to get through this. And you've got to get through it with the least amount of damage to yourself and your daughter. And I think that, you know, maybe between the two of us, we can do that. Are you willing to give it a shot?

Gord: Okay.

Reflections

Needless to say, Adele's confidence in shared parenting was badly shaken. Her suspicion that the only reason her former husband agreed to sharing in the first place was to stay involved with her seemed justified when Margaret began to ask why mother and father couldn't live together again. The situation was deteriorating rapidly, and the only recourse was to interview everyone concerned to determine whether the arrangement could continue and whether Margaret's interests were being served.

Gord admitted that, although he hadn't been completely aware of it at first, he was using shared parenting as a secret avenue for reconciliation. The knowledge that his former wife was committed to another relationship began expressing itself in plans to try for sole custody. Not only was he terrified that another man would replace him as a father, but he was also terribly jealous and bitter.

In this instance it was possible to determine several things: except for relatively minor recent incidents, Margaret was secure within shared parenting, gradually accepting that she was loved and cared for in both households; Adele felt that the situation was positive for her daughter; and Richard was not interested in replacing the child's natural father, although he did care for her.

The Watkins family's arrangement continues. Through mediation, Adele and Richard agreed not to move in together for a period of three months; for his part, Gord promised not to enter into any legal proceedings for the same period of time. This compromise was reached to give Gordon time to accept the idea that the marriage was over but not the parenting.

Shared parenting works when both parents are completely committed to it. If it is to work at all in this instance, Gord must be able to accept it for what it is.

This story illustrates that there are risks in shared parenting and that a great deal of certainty is necessary before it will be workable. Not only that, but considerable attention is required to keep it functioning properly.

In my experience, this is an unusual case; people who are willing to entertain the idea of shared parenting are generally able to recognize the pitfalls beforehand. As I have mentioned, however, shared parenting is not a cure-all.

CASE 3: JEANNE AND GARTH JANSEN

In the following true story the couple was fairly typical in struggling early in the mediation process to develop a mediation mindset, but then moving quickly and smoothly into creating a shared-parenting plan.

CHILDREN COME FIRST

Background

Jeanne Jansen contacted our office on her lawyer's recommendation. She and her husband, Garth, were still living in the same house but were in the process of separating. Their primary concern was the custody, access, and support of their nine-year-old son, Eric, and division of property and assets.

Each wanted sole custody, she said, and was willing to give the other liberal visiting rights. However, tension was high. It was hard for her to assert herself with Garth. She felt overpowered by his anger. She hoped mediation would help Garth understand that his attitude was detrimental and help her to better state her opinions. Garth was agreeable to mediation and Jeanne said she would ask him to contact me, as well. He called the following day.

Individual Interview — Jeanne

Jeanne, forty-three, was a bilingual Francophone who came across as soft-spoken, stressed, and anxious, but articulate. She was a primary-school teacher. Neither spouse had family locally, nor did they have a large circle of friends. Her salary was in the middle-income range. The couple was debt-free, owned two cars, and lived in their own home.

Jeanne told me that she had initiated the marital separation. She felt Garth had been dominant in the marriage and that she had deferred to him. In his family, the male was the head of the family. This was acceptable to her for the first part of the marriage, because Garth was also protective and attentive. But now he was strenuously opposed to the separation and very angry about it.

When Jeanne began evaluating her marriage, she had sought out a therapist at Family Services. She was finding therapy helpful in dealing with her guilt and anger and, although

she was anxious about it, she was beginning to stand up to her husband. She had discussed mediation with her therapist and had consulted her regarding several mediators recommended by her lawyer. She ended up coming to me for mediation.

When I inquired about reconciliation, Jeanne stated clearly that the marriage was over for her and that she needed to get on with her life. She was still living with Garth to ensure that she had a good chance of obtaining custody. When asked about Garth's dominant character and the potential for violence, she indicated that there had been no violence in the past. Although Garth could be angry and abrupt with her, she did not feel he would ever be physically aggressive.

At that point, I asked about Eric's reaction to the tension in the household and the ensuing separation. I asked this question to focus Jeanne's attention on one of the key purposes of mediation — to secure an arrangement that would be in Eric's best interest.

Jeanne described a negative change in Eric's attitude and performance at school. She said he was testing the limits at home and was having nightmares. Eric had been pampered by both his parents in the past. However, Jeanne was concerned that since the decision to separate, Garth was catering to the child, openly blaming her for the separation, and making comments about "boys needing to live with their fathers."

Jeanne was worried about Garth's manipulative behaviour and hoped that he would "hear out" a neutral party. She had trusted his parenting in the past; both parents had adhered to routine and structure. She said Garth and Eric were particularly close.

Individual Interview — Garth

The following day, Garth came in for his initial interview. A fifty-five-year-old accountant, bilingual, and of Armenian extraction, he came across as rational, controlling, and a bit guarded. He had a responsible position in an accounting firm, with a salary higher than Jeanne's. Garth had agreed to come to mediation because his lawyer had recommended it, and he hoped it would save time and expense. When Jeanne asked him if he would meet with the therapist at Family Services, he refused, saying that she was "her therapist." Besides, he was not interested in therapy, but in settling issues.

When I asked Garth how the decision to separate came about, he became less self-assured. It was clear he was quite angry and distraught. He thought their personalities had worked well together, with him acting as the decision-maker because she was so easy-going. He would have been willing to work on their marriage had she talked with him before coming to the decision to separate. Because her mind was made up, he just wanted to ensure that he would not lose his son.

I asked him to describe Eric and his reactions to the situation and Garth spoke at some length about his involvement with his son, his parenting style, and his previous confidence in Jeanne's parenting skills. Garth was concerned about Eric's shaky adjustment.

I turned next to Garth's stress level (high), and especially the few supports and resources available to him.

I had one more session with each partner, attempting to help them understand how they made decisions, managed conflict, and expressed anger. This contributed to the assessment effort, but would also be helpful in setting the stage for negotiations, especially in helping prepare them for their continued relationship as parents.

Joint Interview

The following week, the Jansens came for a joint interview. To keep the process transparent and avoid having either spouse thinking the mediator privy to the other spouse's secrets, I asked each spouse to talk again about how they saw their marital difficulties, how they got started, and what they expected to get out of mediation. When asked who wanted to go first, Garth jumped in immediately, blaming Jeanne for not telling him about her concerns much earlier.

With support and encouragement, Jeanne was able to tell Garth about feeling unheard and overruled by him.

I asked both how these feelings might affect mediation, using this opportunity to pursue both spouses' bottom line, their perception of the process of mediation, and their joint responsibility for the outcome.

Again, Garth expressed anger, but was able to say that he would make an effort to be reasonable during the mediation process.

I asked each spouse to spend some time talking about Eric — how each parented him and how each saw the other spouse's parenting.

I then provided background information about the typical reaction of children to parental separation and the child's need for consistency and protection from parental conflict. I also asked the couple to distinguish between their needs and distress as separating spouses, their ongoing parental roles, and their son's needs. I emphasized their common interest in parenting the child they both loved dearly.

At that point, because they seemed ready to begin mediation, I had them sign the standard mediation contract, which specified the expected rules of conduct, the fee-splitting arrangement, and the understanding that they were responsible for a settlement, which would be ratified by their lawyers rather than by the mediator. In preparation for the next session, I asked them to start thinking about the family's future, especially care of Eric and how they saw their respective roles.

CHILDREN COME FIRST

Pre-Mediation

Three sessions with Garth focused on past marital relationship patterns and gave him an opportunity to express his feelings. The emphasis throughout was on helping him understand that his reactions were normal and reinterpreting his experience to allow him to see it as an opportunity for growth, both as a person and as a parent. In particular, I repeatedly asked him how he intended to parent Eric in the future.

We explored specific parenting skills, separating his needs from those of Eric. Through time, Garth's anger gradually became more diffused. He began to think how he planned to parent Eric, yet not be in complete charge of him. His growing ability to focus on future plans and on his parenting indicated to me that he was ready to move to the next stage of mediation.

I had a long but fruitful session with Jeanne. I supported her in dealing with the stress of cohabitation. I checked on her level of comfort during the previous joint session. Jeanne felt that the ongoing sessions with her therapist were very helpful and she agreed that I could communicate with the therapist if Jeanne felt it necessary.

Then, as with Garth, I discussed with Jeanne how she and Garth intended to parent Eric. This discussion emphasized the importance of separating her feelings for Garth from the shared work they needed to do as parents. That she was able to do so boded well for the next stage of mediation. Furthermore, a call to her therapist indicated that she was working with Jeanne in ways that were supportive of mediation: assertiveness and communication training, as well as support of Jeanne's transition to single parenthood.

Negotiation

With this extensive preparation in place, negotiation was relatively brief and not unusually complicated. At the start of the first session, I stressed the importance of co-operation and mutual trust by asking Jeanne and Garth to recall past experiences when they had worked together successfully on issues concerning parenting. The couple came up with several examples, which helped to establish a positive tone to the meeting.

As negotiation proper began, I first established a structure for the spouses by setting the agenda. The spouses agreed that their main concern was custody, access, and child support. However, previous discussion had made it clear that these were emotionally charged issues and would likely be difficult. In contrast, Garth indicated that property division was less important to him, although Jeanne expressed some apprehension about equity in this area, because her salary was less than Garth's.

Both partners were able to discuss their wishes and agreed that the family home would be sold and the proceeds divided proportionately. They agreed on the division of the furniture, with each keeping the car they now used. Pension funds and Garth's investments would be divided proportionately. Lawyers were involved in the financial matters.

As the session ended, I emphasized how well the couple had worked together to arrive at these reasonable and fair decisions, expressed confidence that they would continue to so, and asked them to confer with their lawyers on these matters.

In the next session we focused on parenting issues. To avoid conflict, much time was spent clarifying and extending the spouses' parenting options. This process involved exploring the success other couples had had with shared parenting, the values that typically underpinned this choice, and what it might entail on a day-to-day basis. As expected, the partners had a variety of questions. I ended the session by asking them to think carefully about their specific options and the likely consequences of each, and to bring their ideas to the next session.

Garth was looking for an apartment, while Jeanne would remain in the home until it was sold. Garth agreed to pay his share of the costs of maintenance and repair work needed to ready the house for sale. Discussion throughout was relatively cordial, even positive, although Garth had to be reminded to give Jeanne equal air time, and Jeanne needed occasional support in expressing her views.

In closing, I asked them to write out a draft agreement in their own words. This was forwarded to their respective lawyers. I followed up by calling each lawyer to explain the process by which the agreement was arrived at and its intent. The lawyers approved the agreement with a few minor amendments. Jeanne's lawyer translated it into legal terminology and this version was signed by both spouses.

Follow-Up

I met with Jeanne and Garth six months later. Despite minor changes, their agreement was still basically intact and seemed to be working well. They had been able to resolve minor parenting disagreements by themselves. As at the end of negotiation, I closed the session by telling them to expect occasional difficulties in the future but expressed confidence that they had the ability to handle it on their own. I told them that should they encounter more serious difficulties, they could be assured that my door was always open to them.

The Jansens were clearly on their way to an ongoing and consistent shared-parenting arrangement.

6

Principles and Guidelines for Creating Shared-Parenting Plans

Each child has the right to have two homes where he or she is cherished and given the opportunity to develop normally.[21]
— Isolina Ricci

In the previous chapter we looked at the shift in society's view of divorce from parent-centred to child-centred, and from custody as a way of dealing with the children to shared parenting. We then went through the experience of mediation that culminates in shared-parenting plans by going through real-life stories from my practice.

In this chapter I will focus on the main principles to be followed when you construct a parenting plan, as well as certain guidelines. I will show you how to create your own plan. Understanding and committing to these principles and guidelines will make your own shared-parenting plan better, stronger, and longer lasting.

FIRST PRINCIPLES IN CONSTRUCTING PARENTING PLANS

Following are the main principles of strong parenting plans, based on the writing and research of Isolina Ricci.[22]

1. **The children are the primary owners of the relationship with their parents.**
   Traditional discussions of child custody and access have focused heavily on the individual rights of parents. Such rights may or may not coincide with the best interests of the children.

2. **Children and their parents have certain rights in divorce.**

   - Each child has the right to have two homes where he or she is cherished and given the opportunity to develop normally.
   - Each child has a right to a meaningful, nurturing relationship with each parent.
   - Each parent and child has the right to call themselves a family, regardless of how the children's time is divided.
   - Each parent has the responsibility and the right to share in raising his or her children.
   - Each child has the right to have competent parents and to be free from hearing, observing, or being caught up in their parents' arguments or problems with each other.
   - Each parent has the right to his or her own private life and territory — the new family boundary — and to raise the children without unreasonable interference by the other parent.

Regardless of their particular arrangement, both parents share in the responsibility of caring for their children. This is not because they have a right to do, so but because their mutual involvement aids their children's healthy development. This principle, however, comes with an important qualification: that such involvement serves the needs of children only so long as it builds a firewall between those needs and the parents' marital difficulties.

Finally, these rights recognize that divorce does not mean the end of the family system but rather its reorganization into two subsystems, each with its own separate boundary. So long as the parenting that goes on within each subsystem keeps the children from risk, it should be allowed to continue without interference by the other parent.

3. **Each child is unique.**
Although children have needs in common, each is in some ways unique, with an individual blend of strengths and weaknesses — some constitutional, others environmental. This principle recognizes that a parenting arrangement that works well for one child may be harmful to another. It is the responsibility of parents in divorce to construct parenting plans that recognize and acknowledge such differences in their children.

4. **A good legal agreement cannot guarantee a good result.**
Parenting agreements arrived at through litigation vary widely. Some are good agreements that are fair and sensitive to the needs of the children, but others are bad agreements that are neither fair nor sensitive to the children. However, irrespective of their quality, such agreements cannot and do not teach parents

how to get along in a positive and constructive way, nor do they tell parents how to maintain a supportive and loving relationship with their children. Such agreements are important because they formalize parenting arrangements after divorce, but they are insufficient in and of themselves to ensure that children will be protected and allowed to develop normally.

5. **How parents relate to each other after separation is crucial.**
One of the most potent predictors of child development after divorce is the way parents relate to each other in front of the children. The children who are least affected by their parents' divorce have parents who allow them to have a loving and supportive relationship with each parent and systematically exclude the children from adult matters, including conflict. The children whose development is impaired, perhaps permanently, following divorce are those whose parents compete for their affection, engage in destructive conflict in front of them, or encourage them to take sides in the conflict.[23]

6. **As the "executives" of their family, adults make the final decisions.**
Healthy families are organized hierarchically, with a clear separation between the roles played by parents and children. Executive functions — that is, adult issues and final decisions regarding parenting — are the parents' sole responsibility. Although children can and should be encouraged to have a say in decisions affecting them, the final decisions should always rest with their parents. Children's responsibilities increase with age and involve the range of issues associated with normal growth and development, including

social relations with family members, peers, and others, and the work and play associated with curricular and extracurricular activities.

7. **Divorce precipitates a confrontation with many traditional values and beliefs.**

The divorce rate in North America has ensured the destruction of the negative stereotypes previously associated with divorce. Even so, on an individual basis, parents may still emerge from divorce feeling that they have failed at two of life's primary adult tasks: marriage and parenting. As part of their education as parents in and following divorce, parents must come to realize that although their marriage has ended, their family continues to survive in a different form.

Parents must also accept that they have an ongoing responsibility to be good parents to their children, even if that means disposing of traditional notions of parenting. That is, both parents can continue to parent well despite the fact that they live in different households, may need to learn to relate to the other parent in new ways, and may even have new partners.

8. **There is such a thing as a sensible divorce, and it is worth the effort to get it.**

A sensible divorce is a shorthand way of speaking about a structural model of a healthy family in divorce. That model encompasses four primary features:

- As mentioned above, adult issues and parenting decisions are left solely in the hands of the parents as family "executives," with the children excluded from such affairs and from anything to do with parenting conflict and hostility.

- There are two separate bounded households involving each parent and the children, with each parent free to carry on with normal parenting, with the flexible support of the other parent.
- The parents develop a positive, constructive, and business-like relationship characterized by co-operation, mutual respect, negotiation, and effective problem-solving.
- The children are encouraged to have a loving and supportive relationship with each parent, with the approval and support of the other parent.

PRACTICAL GUIDELINES FOR ENACTING PARENTING PLANS

Taken together, the above principles set out the goals and objectives of healthy parenting in divorce. However, for many parents in divorce, especially those caught up in a cycle of destructive conflict and hostility, these principles are inadequate because they fail to specify how these goals are to be achieved.

You may find yourself in this situation, wanting specifics in how to approach your parenting plan. For advice in enacting these principles, I turn to the following practical guidelines, based on my own experience and the accumulated wisdom of Ricci[24] and centred mostly on the co-parenting relationship and the relationship between parents and children in divorce. These are offered as guidelines only. Parents in divorce may have other ways to achieve desirable outcomes for themselves and their children. Mediators can help parents formulate them and can include them as an appendix to the parents' Memorandum of Understanding.

1. **Parents should strive for a decent, businesslike working relationship with each other that meets the needs of their children.**[25]

    • Watch your language; be courteous and mutually respectful.
    • Keep your feelings in check.
    • Respect the other parent's privacy and expect the same in return.
    • Act like a guest in the other parent's home.
    • Don't expect appreciation or praise from the other parent, but do acknowledge when your partner shows understanding, sensitivity or compromises.
    • Keep a positive but realistic attitude.
    • Keep your sense of humour and encourage the same in the other parent.
    • Be reliable; do what you say you're going to do, and expect the same from the other parent.
    • Be flexible and supportive of the other parent and expect the same in return.
    • Be patient; Rome wasn't built in a day.
    • Expect to feel strange about this new relationship at first; give yourself time to adjust.
    • Though it may be difficult at first, don't give up; the effort is worth it.

For you and the other parent to develop and maintain a positive, constructive, and co-operative relationship you must both begin behaving like colleagues or business associates. That is, you should be moderate in your language and conduct, be positive in your outlook and expectations, focus on a series of shared projects or tasks, and work as a team toward shared goals and objectives.

Such relationships take time to "gel" and so may feel odd or awkward at first, feelings that gradually fade with experience.

Because of inevitable start-up problems, such efforts require patience and perseverance because the stakes are very high indeed: the present and future well-being of your children. If you succeed, as many can and will do, that future is as assured — any set of loving parents can make it. If you fail, because you are continuing to be caught up in a cycle of negative intimacy, that future is likely to be compromised.

2. **In all interactions with the other parent, use good communication practices.**[26]

- Be explicit with the other parent.
- Communicate directly with the other parent at all times; never use the children to send messages to the other parent.
- Say what you mean and mean what you say; make no assumptions.
- Double-check your verbal understandings; to build trust, be sure to avoid taking the other parent for granted.
- Demonstrate you understand what the other parent is saying.
- Try to ensure that verbal and non-verbal messages are the same and not in conflict.
- Know the things that trigger conflict between you and the other parent and avoid them.
- Confront only with great care.
- Keep the other parent a person in your mind; don't make him or her into a "monster."

One of the key aspects of any businesslike relationship is how effectively the parties communicate — obviously not through the trading of insults or engaging in shouting matches but through regular, consistent, and respectful sharing of information. You and your spouse may not have developed good communication skills. That doesn't mean it's too late to learn them. The mediation process can help you develop them for the sake of your children. Following a business model helps. Unlike friends or lovers, who know each other well, business colleagues know each other superficially and so must work hard to ensure that they consistently communicate clearly. Among other things, this means that communication — both verbal and non-verbal messages — is direct (excluding third parties), explicit, and congruent. As good "business partners," be sure to

- avoid forms of communication (such as sarcasm or irony) that might obscure meaning;
- check that the right message has been received by the other; and
- acknowledge receipt of the message from the other.

Effective business communication restricts confrontation and proceeds cautiously, mindful of the need for periodic relationship repair. Such repair includes a mental portrait of the other as a person, like oneself, doing his or her best under conditions that are stressful and often very trying — a good model for parenting after divorce.

3. **Work as parents to maintain a healthy, positive parenting pattern.**[27]

- Time with the children is time together, not babysitting.
- Make your children's needs more important than your territorial rights or your independence; always put children before rules or procedures.
- Respect the other parent's time with the children.
- Respect the other parent's parenting style.
- Interfere with the other parent's effort only if your children need your protection.

- Share information about the children frequently with the other parent; parenting continuity is important as the children move between households.
- Parents should compare notes on the other adults in your children's lives, including teachers, coaches, medical and dental professionals, and others.
- Each parent should be supportive of the other parent's relationship with the children.
- Don't use the children to carry messages to the other parent.

Do your best to go beyond grudging acceptance or guarded tolerance of the other parent's involvement with the children. Actually encourage and promote such relations because they are good for the children. Respect boundaries and accept the other parent's parenting style, even if he or she does things with the children that you might not do. Open and maintain a one-on-one dialogue that enables both of you to share information with each other, so that you are equally up to date on what is happening with and to their your children.

This open attitude may mean sacrificing your territorial and other rights, or compromising on issues where you know you are "right." Conflict over these issues is not good for the children.

4. **Work as parents to develop and maintain a healthy, positive relationship with your children.**[28]

- Let your children know that you are thinking about them and expect them to keep in touch with you.
- Talk to your children regularly; young children in particular need to understand the changes in their lives in ways that are visible, touchable, and concrete.
- Give children a say in the decisions that affect their lives. Ensure that they feel heard, even though, as you make clear, adults make all final decisions.

- Don't bad-mouth the other parent in the presence of the children.
- Do not participate in the children's angry feelings about the other parent.
- Encourage the children to speak about any difficulties they are having with the other parent, but do not pursue it at length; suggest other adults in whom the child might wish to confide.
- Do not ask the children about the other parent's life or circumstances; respect the other parent's privacy and give his or her motives the benefit of any doubt.
- Do not tell the children to keep secrets about you from the other parent.
- Be the grown-up; avoid leaning on the children to satisfy your need for support, encouragement, and/or care.
- Keep changes to a minimum during the first few years, especially if the children are very young.
- Never threaten to abandon your children.
- Know and respond to danger signals in your children and get help as required.
- Provide your children with structure and predictability.
- Don't lead your children to believe that you may reconcile with the other parent.
- Calm your children's fears and help rebuild trust and security.
- Frequently reassure the children of your love and that you will always be there to care for them and look after their needs.

The process of divorce is not only hard on the adults; it is just as hard or harder on the children. Their healthy development depends on knowing that their parents will always be there for them, that their needs will be met, and that they will continue to be loved and cherished by both parents. It also depends on the knowledge that both parents will continue to function as parents; that is, that they will behave like adults, speak honestly about the divorce, address the children's fears and concerns, and maintain those family rules and routines that have given the children's lives order, structure, and meaning.

As a parent you should remember that each child is unique and may respond to the demands of the divorcing process quite differently than his or her brothers or sisters, even though they may be quite close in age. It is the responsibility of you and the other parent to be sensitive to any danger signals indicating that a child is in distress and to get that child whatever help is needed.

And be prepared for your own reaction to periodic separations from your children. The late Frederick C. Gans, barrister, brings sharply into focus the emotional pain felt by the parent who, when divorcing, must move away from his or her children, in an article entitled "The Non-Custodial Parent: A Personal View."[29]

> Separation by a father or a mother from his or her kids involves a number of things. For example, the noise at breakfast and at dinner, the stream of questions as to how high is up and things of that nature, the apple juice crawling its sticky way across the kitchen floor, all of these things are terminated very quickly. These little elements that we as parents seem to take for granted when our children are with us are suddenly taken away and the non-custodial parent is met with nothing but deafening silence in his apartment.
>
> But in addition, implicit in the loss of custody is the loss of the right to govern the day-to-day activities and destinies of the child; the right to share with the child the hundreds of experiences that comprise his daily existence. He misses the millions of little things such as the hugs and the kisses, the dirty faces and the

scuffed knees and elbows, and the privilege of tucking the child into bed at night and receiving a mushy kiss on the snoot and a "Goodnight."

5. Consider including your children in forming the parenting plan.

"In a twenty-five-year follow-up study of the responses of children and adolescents to parental separation and divorce, Wallerstein and Lewis found that these adults recalled feeling that they had been silenced and expected, without recourse, to follow visiting or custody plans that had not been made with their wishes in mind."[30]

It's not that children should feel omnipotent and make decisions about the parenting plan, but that they should be *heard and considered* regarding their wishes. The final decision should rest with the parent.

Sometimes I will invite the children to attend one or more sessions. This can be especially positive when one of you is unable or unwilling to "hear" the other parent with regard to his or her relationship with the children. In addition, involving the children can help you move the process along because the children may be more likely to do their part later in making the plan work.

Donald Saposnek, a highly respected family mediator, writes about helping parents prepare their children for an interview with the mediator:

"The way in which the parents frame the request to a child to come in for an interview can make a big difference in the validity of the child's report. For example, imagine the effects on a child whose parent prepares him for the interview with something like the following:

143

Next Tuesday, I'm taking you to the mediator that Mom and Dad are seeing. He's going
to ask you to tell him who you want to live
with. Honey, don't forget to tell him that you
want to live with me or the judge might take
you away from me and not let me see you ever
again. I really love you, so be sure to tell the
mediator that you want to live with me.

This child is likely to believe that he will be asked
to choose which parent he loves more — a very scary
proposition that generates a forced conflict of loyalty
and much resulting anxiety. The child will likely feel
frightened, intimidated, and reluctant to reveal honest feelings or opinions to the mediator.

In contrast, consider the effect of the following
statement:

Your [mother/father] and I have been talking with a mediator about how we're going to
share our time with you when we live separately. We both love you very much, and we
would like you to help us understand your
feelings about the arrangements for spending
time with each of us so that we can make better decisions for you. Our mediator is really
nice and easy to talk with. He talks with lots
of children and helps lots of moms and dads
who are getting divorced understand their
children's feelings. So we'd both like for you
to talk with him so he can help us as a family.[31]

Obviously in the second situation, the child would
feel supported and be in a state of readiness to talk
openly and honestly with the mediator. In fact, I have

found many children feel relieved when they are able to talk about their concerns following the separation.

Even when the mediator has decided not to include the children, there is another option — to include them symbolically. Children can be brought into the session by a particular questioning technique. For example, each parent separately may be asked by the mediator to describe the children. Subsequent questions may make that description as detailed as your mediator thinks necessary. Tell me what your children are like? *What sort of things do they enjoy doing? What do they say that makes you laugh?*

Supplementary questions can also invoke the children's presence in session *How would you like your children to speak about you [or the other parent] when looking back on this time ten years from now [or when they turn eighteen, or as an adult]?*

Recently, I worked with parents who came into a mediation session with four 5 x 7 framed photographs of their children. They put the pictures on my coffee table and said, "This is why we're here today." It certainly caused me to focus far more intensely on the best interests of their beautiful children.

7

How to Create *Your* Shared-Parenting Plan

Children of divorce do best in the short- and long-run when they feel loved and cared for by both parents. This is most likely to occur when the children have ongoing contact with both parents, who participate fully in their lives.

The basic elements of all parenting plans include where the children will live, how they will share time with each parent, how major decisions will be made about their care, how parents will deal with changes in circumstances, and how the parents will deal with future impasses.

All plans must specify how the children will spend time with each of their parents. Your parenting plan can be customized to suit what works best for your children, taking into consideration their developmental stages and their schedules.

In the interests of clarity, we will distinguish between routine or daily schedules and holiday schedules, deferring discussion of the latter to the next section. Although preferred arrangements will certainly vary across North American jurisdictions, some of the more common in our experience are the following:

5/14 Alternating Schedule with Midweek Overnight

This first one does not fully qualify as a shared-parenting plan. It is more like a sole custody situation. However, there are cases when shared parenting takes this shape, usually when the mother is at home and the father, because of business, is unable to care for the children more intensively. This is a typical schedule in such a case:

Monday	Tuesday	Wednesday	Thursday	Friday	Saturday	Sunday
Mom	Mom	Dad	Mom	Dad	Dad	Dad
Mom	Mom	Dad	Mom	Dad	Dad	Dad
Mom	Mom	Dad	Mom	Mom	Mom	Mom
Mom	Mom	Dad	Mom	Mom	Mom	Mom

50/50 Shared-Parenting Options — Alternating Weeks

(This plan is typically for older children.)

Monday	Tuesday	Wednesday	Thursday	Friday	Saturday	Sunday
Mom	Mom	Mom	Mom	Dad	Dad	Dad
Mom	Mom	Mom	Mom	Dad	Dad	Dad
Dad	Dad	Dad	Dad	Mom	Mom	Mom
Dad	Dad	Dad	Dad	Mom	Mom	Mom

50/50 Shared-Parenting Options — Five-Day/Two-Day Rotation

Monday	Tuesday	Wednesday	Thursday	Friday	Saturday	Sunday
Mom	Mom	Dad	Dad	Mom	Mom	Mom
Mom	Mom	Dad	Dad	Mom	Mom	Mom
Mom	Mom	Dad	Dad	Dad	Dad	Dad
Mom	Mom	Dad	Dad	Dad	Dad	Dad

THE FIVE ELEMENTS OF GOOD
SHARED-PARENTING PLANS

Good parenting plans also include five additional concerns:

1. **Mom's house, Dad's house:**
    The first concern is *where* your children will live. The usual arrangement is one in which each parent has separate accommodations, with the children moving back and forth between homes. Under special circumstances, however, parents have been known to prefer a "bird's nest" arrangement, in which the children remain in the matrimonial home and the *parents* move in and out for specified intervals.

    For this to work, both of you must have separate accommodations when you are not with the children. This choice is usually a transitional one, while one or both parents search for new accommodations as the matrimonial home is being sold, for example. Typically, this may work for only a short period of time.

    Still another variation is one in which all family members remain in the matrimonial home, with each parent living on different floors. This variation is usually temporary, in place while a parenting plan is being negotiated. It ensures that the parent who then leaves the matrimonial home and establishes a new household is not seen by the courts as having "abandoned" the children.

2. **Pickups and drop-offs:**
    The second concern relates to the transition process, that is, which parent is responsible for transporting the children from one parent to the other.

    One variation involves travel by both parents, with the resident parent responsible for transporting the children to the home of the non-resident parent.

A second variation involves the use of third parties, such as teachers, daycare providers, or babysitters from whom a parent can pick up the children or who may volunteer to transport the children to a parent. When both parents work, as is often the case, transfer can be between third parties, for example, from a daycare provider to a babysitter who cares for the children until a parent gets home from work.

A third variation involves one of the parents being responsible for all transportation between homes. In some cases, this variation reflects the fact that only one parent has access to a vehicle and/or that the other parent has certain driving preferences, such as avoiding any night-time travel. More often, this variation reflects an unequal relationship between the parents.

3. **Try to be on time:**
   The third concern relates to the timing of transition points, that is, when transitions are scheduled to occur. Most child-sharing schedules reflect parents' work schedules, the children's school schedule, or both. As a result, pickup and drop-off times are typically before school, after work, or both. More variations can be found when transitions occur on the weekend.

   In all cases, transition points

   - usually refer to specific times, such as 8:00 a.m.;
   - include some definition of what late means, with "on time" often referring to a ten- to fifteen-minute interval (such as 8:00 to 8:15 a.m.) rather than a point in time, to take account of unexpected delays;
   - assume "due notice" when the parent doing the pickup or drop-off is going to be late; and
   - include some understanding about what is to happen at transition (for example, that the

children will be ready to go; that any conversation between the parents be of a limited duration, such as five or ten minutes; and that such conversations be confined to matters concerning the children) (see below).

4. **A co-operative relationship:**
Another issue relates to the content of conversation during transition points and highlights the importance of a co-operative relationship. Parents in conflict have often broken off communication by the time they enter family mediation. Rather than parenting together, they are actually parenting in parallel. This is often dysfunctional and makes for very inefficient parenting. It is also very hard on the children because both parents must "start over" with the children, unaware of what has transpired in their absence.

Children benefit from knowing their parents are talking about them and care enough to share information about them. To begin the arduous task of recreating dialogue between parents, transition points can offer an ideal opportunity. Accordingly, at each transition the resident parent may be required to list for the other parent, in summary form, the highlights of the children's time with him or her. These highlights can vary widely, concerning time at home, time at school, time with friends, time with relatives, health issues, and so on. The other parent is to receive this report without comment, save for any clarifying questions and a brief thank-you for the information (see Parental Communication below).

5. **Sharing children during the holidays and special events:**
Daily family routine is broken up by holidays and various special events.

Among school-age children, holidays include summer vacation and various statutory or religious holidays such as Christmas, New Year's, Easter, and Thanksgiving.

Special events may be tied to quasi-official events, such as Mother's Day, Father's Day, March Break, or Halloween, or may be family-related, such as birthdays or anniversaries. Special events may also be tied to cultural norms and conventions, for example, Ramadan, Kwanza, Rosh Hashanah, Yom Kippur, or Passover. Families in divorce can vary widely as to which of these holidays and special events they choose to honour; however, it would be quite rare for families to honour none of them.

You need to handle these times with care. They are often hotly contested. It is not uncommon, for example, for litigation to focus on child-sharing during Christmas. Thus, holidays and special events are a standard feature of parenting plans, and the following variations in sharing arrangements are commonplace:

Annual Rotation: One variation involves annual rotation. For example, in Year 1, the children may spend Christmas Eve with the mother, Christmas Day with the father, and New Year's Day with the mother. In Year 2, the arrangement reverses, with the children spending Christmas Eve with the father and so on.

In addition, holiday schedules come with an important proviso — namely, that for specified holidays or special events, the regular schedule is suspended. This is important because conflict can erupt if special events fall on either parent's "regular day." Because rotating schedules cross years, use of a sixteen-month calendar to mark off the days can avoid later confusion or conflict.

Annual Alternation: A second variation involves annual alteration. For example, in Year 1 the children will go out for Halloween with the mother. In Year 2 they will go out with the father.

Alternation, then, is logistically less complex than rotation and requires less interaction between the parents. However, it also involves less contact between the children and each parent and is thus less desirable from a developmental perspective.

In practical terms, the choice between rotation and alteration usually depends on the degree to which you can tolerate interaction with your former spouse.

Planning Holidays in Advance: Finally, some occasions will require advance notice from one parent to the other. For example, the precise time when each parent takes his or her summer vacation may vary from year to year. To avoid confusion and possible overlap, a parenting plan will require each parent to notify the other of vacation plans six to eight weeks in advance and often in writing. The same applies should such plans involve foreign travel. Here, notice should be accompanied by a written itinerary, including dates, places, and emergency telephone numbers.

Such requests for information should not be seen as intrusive but as prudent in the case of unforeseen events. Furthermore, note that the parent doing the travelling will typically require a consent letter from the other parent to clear customs.

PARENTAL AND ROUTINE DECISION-MAKING

In two-parent families, the parents — *and only the parents* — are the executives charged with making decisions about all important matters affecting the children. Although parents can and should consult the children as to their wishes and opinions, as well as others (such as teachers, grandparents, and friends), the final decision is theirs and theirs alone.

Furthermore, the process of arriving at such decisions should be held strictly in private and certainly out of the earshot of the children. Once such decisions have been arrived at, they will be conveyed to the children with the understanding that they are *no longer negotiable.*

This approach to decision-making recognizes that too often children become part of the power struggle between parents, and they are simply unequipped to avoid being caught in a loyalty bind. On one hand, parents are often unaware of such binds, simply blaming the other parent for their irresponsible behaviour. On the other hand, such binds can be highly destructive to children.

The rule of executive decision-making is intended to remove the children from the loop. That said, child involvement in age- and gender-appropriate decisions facilitates their normal development. The notion of *routine* decisions attempts to capture this aspect of child rearing. Thus, although children would never be asked if they want a medical operation, they could be asked to choose between a teddy bear and a toy truck as the toy they want to take with them to the hospital. Similarly, they might be asked to choose between a red T-shirt and a green T-shirt when they are choosing their clothes for school the next day. Thus, parents set the limits, but the children are free to act within these limits.

This arrangement makes for clear rules of authority within families of divorce, with parents alone responsible for major decisions and children responsible for those minor decision that affect them. Furthermore, a child's routine decisions should become increasingly significant with advancing age and maturity. Among teenagers, for example, executive decision-making will gradually shade into intergenerational negotiation. This is an entirely appropriate way to teach children about responsible decision-making, such that they will be ready to take on this responsibility in adulthood.

CHILDREN'S EDUCATION

If you have toddler-aged children, educational concerns will focus on babysitting, daycare, and preschool. With school-aged children, the focus shifts to academic programs, remedial programs, academic achievement, relations with teachers and other school staff, and the choice of school district. With adolescents, the focus shifts again to vocational concerns, college preparation, college funding, and the transition from one school system to another (see Extracurricular Activities, page 157).

Each of these issues involves shared responsibility, as well as the need for parental dialogue and negotiation, and thus bears the potential for conflict. For example, it is preferable that parents attend parent-teacher meetings together, though separate meetings can be arranged if need be. The consent of both parents will be required should the children require remedial help and/or testing.

The same will be true with regard to vocational or special programs, such as driver's education. It is important that children not be used as couriers between parents. Each of you as parents should make your own independent arrangements to get school notices, report cards, school records, and the like. Continuity is also to your child's advantage when it comes to homework and work on special assignments or projects.

All of these issues require parental co-operation in the best interest of the child. Creating a parenting plan will walk you through these and other, more specialized issues concerned with education.

CHILDREN'S HEALTH CARE

A second area of joint decision-making concerns health care. Care of minor injuries or illnesses will be the responsibility of the resident parent alone. However, both of you should be informed of your children's medical records, medical and dental appointments, and medical and dental treatments, including drugs and antibiotics, orthodontic or endodontic care, specialized nutritional regimens, and the need for invasive treatments, such as surgery.

Both of you should be involved as much as possible in medical decision-making, although the resident parent should be invested with the authority to make emergency decisions regarding a child's health care. Furthermore, treatment regimens absolutely require parenting continuity and thus co-operation. For example, a ten-day antibiotic regimen means that the medicine travels with the child from one household to the other.

More generally, your parenting plan will set out the following guideline: the children's best interest supersedes routine time-sharing arrangements. For example, children who are ill should not be made to travel, and a parent who is ill should not receive the children, whether or not it is "your" time with them.

In practice, this means that sick children, because they do not transport well and for their own safety, should be left in the care of the resident parent, even if this disrupts the routine time-sharing arrangement temporarily. The same is true when you or the other parent is ill and may infect the children coming into your care. In both cases, such unexpected changes typically do not involve makeup time because they can occur when the children are with either of you, although makeup time may be offered on consent.

RELIGIOUS UPBRINGING

Religious upbringing is a third area where both of you should be involved in decision-making.

The gradual decline of religion across North America means that, a number of cases, parental religious affiliation will be nominal. If that is true of you, religious upbringing is not likely to become a major issue in dispute. Your parenting plan can indicate your agreement that both of you will be will be free to instruct the children in keeping with the religious affiliation in place prior to the separation.

If your family is more traditional, both you and your spouse can agree to carry on the religious tradition in place prior to the divorce. Keep in mind that for devout families, religious instruction can raise a series of hotly contested issues, including the regularity of attendance at religious services, the particular location of religious worship, and the identity of those providing religious instruction.

One variation involves families marked by religious conversion (for example, a Christian woman who converts to marry a Jewish man) or reversion to the person's original faith. Another variation involves devout parents who, on divorce, choose either a less religious form of worship within the same faith or reject the faith altogether.

If you are involved in any such cases, mediation and the development of a shared-parenting plan may face various difficulties. It is a challenge for parents to find a middle ground where value-based differences are concerned, whether the details refer to child-related education, health care, or religious instruction. However difficult it may be to come to an agreement through mediation, at least you as parents have control over the outcome. By contrast, through litigation you would be rendered helpless, at the mercy of an adjudicator who may not share either of your values.

EXTRACURRICULAR EVENTS AND ACTIVITIES

Extracurricular events and activities are a regular feature of the lives of many children. However, in families in which parents live apart, such activities can pose logistical and monetary challenges. In turn, such activities can constitute a fertile breeding ground for conflict between parents. To avoid such conflict requires careful planning, good communication, and clear rules of engagement.

Week-Over-Week Arrangements and Mutual Consent

Family boundaries mean that both parents should be able to raise their children as they see fit on their own time, free of interference from the other parent. In the area of extracurricular activities, this reasoning suggests the following guideline: that *neither parent may commit to week-over-week activities for the children except on mutual consent.* Thus, each parent should be free to enroll a child in any one activity without the other parent's consent, providing (a) the child is willing to become involved, (b) it does not place the child at physical or emotional risk (it is appropriate to the child's age and ability level), and (c) the activity is confined to that parent's time with the child.

To do otherwise would be to violate the guideline concerning respect for boundaries. Moreover, each parent's choice is limited to one activity to avoid inadvertently overburdening the children. However, this clearly limits the activities in which the children may become involved. Many activities, such as sports, dance, or music, for example, require weekly attendance and thus cross week-over-week boundaries. To proceed, such activities require mutual consent that can only arise out of mutual dialogue.

Unexpected Events

Despite carefully laid plans for sharing the children, life sometimes intervenes. Business trips may arise unexpectedly, babysitters or daycare providers may be unavailable, severe weather or labour disruptions may block scheduled vacations, and so on. Although parenting plans cannot foresee every conceivable event, they can be used to set out guidelines and procedures that anticipate these events, thus reducing conflict when they inevitably occur.

PARENTS AS PREFERRED CAREGIVERS

The complexity of your lives may require other caregivers to be called in, either routinely or on an occasional basis. Sometimes these caregivers are family members such as grandparents, aunts, or uncles. Other times they may be daycare providers or babysitters. There is no question that in most cases they provide perfectly adequate care. However, their choice may be problematic when it is made merely to fulfill the obligations of the resident parent, while the other parent is ready and willing to take up the responsibility, despite the fact that he or she is not obliged to do so. Thus, the choice of caregiver does not turn on the quality of care but rather on the quality of the parent-child relationship.

Maintaining or enhancing that relationship will be to the children's developmental advantage. It follows that when a choice is available *on a purely voluntary basis*, parents should be preferred over other caregivers. However, that preference is not an obligation. One of the key advantages of a shared-parenting arrangement is that each parent has some time away from the children. Furthermore, it is increasingly the case that both parents work, often making the need for third-party caregivers unavoidable. Even when the other parent is available to take the children, he or she may not wish to do so. Under these conditions, a third-party caregiver is the obvious choice. However, when the other parent is available and would be willing to take the children, they should be the preferred caregiver.

First Right of Refusal

When the resident parent is unable to look after the children for a period of overnight or more, he or she must offer the other parent the opportunity to look after the children first. If that parent is unable to look after the children, then the resident parent is obligated to make alternate arrangements for the care of the children.

MOVING HOUSEHOLDS

A common feature of parents' complex lives is the occasional need to move from one residence to another. Understandably, long-distance moves can materially affect the time-sharing arrangement and thus can become the focus of intensive negotiation, if not heated dispute.

Such cases may cause you to enter or re-enter into mediation. In most cases a parenting plan can easily be revised and accepted by both parents. Again, it's best to stay within the mediation system where you as parents are in control, as opposed to letting a judge roll the dice.

One helpful way to avoid this situation is to include a mobility provision in a detailed parenting plan. The provision should spell out the conditions of an impending move and state that neither parent will move the children out of an area that would compromise the children from seeing the other parent.

SPECIAL CIRCUMSTANCES

Families entering mediation are alike in many respects, hence the list of standard elements discussed above. However, they are also different or unique in a variety of ways. These unique issues must also be reflected in your parenting plan. It would be impossible to cover here all the variables that may be involved. However, a handful of elements come up with sufficient regularity and deserve special mention.

The Importance of Grandparents

"Grandparents of divorce, like children of divorce, have hardly any legal rights and are voiceless. This is also true of other extended family members. We have not focused enough attention on the part that grandparents can play in the lives of their grandchildren during and after the wrenching experience we call divorce. Love comes in many shades. The love of a grandparent for a grandchild is something very special. It is a love that connects the child with the deeper roots parents provide.

"Reasonable visitation should apply to grandparents just as it applies to parents. Just as we say parents are forever and families are forever, grandparents are also forever and should be acknowledged and recognized as such in the divorce process."[32]

The saying "It Takes a Village" clearly applies to children whose parents have separated.

Same-Sex Partners

It should be noted that the same principles that apply to heterosexual partners apply to same-sex partners. As a matter of fact, mediation tends to be the preferred choice for same-sex partners because the legal alternatives are confusing, and in many states and provinces undeveloped. In my practice, and in discussions with my colleagues, the number of referrals regarding same-sex partners has increased greatly over the past few years.

Family Pets

Pets are often considered an important part of the family. If possible, when separating, family pets should be allowed to move with the children from one parent's home to the other. This is especially meaningful for children who are facing losses and the family pet is very important to them.

The Role of New Partners

Among the issues in contention between divorcing parents, the involvement of a new partner can be especially contentious. This issue involves twin concerns — namely, the means by which these relationships arise and the fears that such relationships promote.

The first and by far the most traumatic scenario that can occur is if a partner has had an affair that may have been one of the catalysts responsible for the breakdown of the marriage. In such cases, the victimized parent is often intensely angry and hurt by the other parent's betrayal while suffering a deep sense of loss and sadness by the disruption of the relationship. In response, he or she may be unwilling even to consider having the new partner come anywhere near the children. There also may be some concerns about the other parent's conduct with the new partner, such as overt sexuality, which may be harmful if witnessed by the children.

Another variation may crop up after the separation, when a stable arrangement is threatened by the new romantic involvement of one of the parents. In this context, the new romantic relationship reawakens feelings of attachment in the other parent — feelings that they themselves may not have been aware were there.

Standard fears here include the possibility that the new partner will take their place in the eyes of their children. This fear is especially prominent in fathers whose former partners have new romantic attachments.

The other common fear is that a child may have been exposed to the new partner too quickly, when the stability of the new relationship has not yet been established. As a matter of fact, approximately 70 percent of remarriages end up in divorce. In this situation, a child may be put at risk, becoming attached to the new partner only to lose that connection when the relationship breaks down. Such losses, coming on the heels of the divorce, can be destructive and affect a child's long-term well-being.

I once had a client, Ken Gaston, whose wife complained to me in mediation that the children were introduced to his new girlfriend as someone that he was considering to marry.

I informed Ken that if the relationship did not last, the children would suffer another loss.

Ken responded, "Dr. Irving, you can tell my wife that if I break up with my girlfriend, Melanie, I'll get another one who looks just like her."

I explained to Ken that girlfriends were not like goldfish that he could replace unbeknownst to the children.

I recommend that you date for at least four to six months before involving your child in a new relationship. Children bond easily and may fantasize that the parent will marry the new partner. After all, this is the model of relationship that the child knew before the divorce. Also, children need one-on-one time with each parent following separation. Since new romantic relationships require an investment of time, that need can compete with the needs of the children. As a result, children can sometimes feel neglected and jealousy can arise.

"If we focus on our children's needs following a separation or divorce we will hopefully slow down and keep our perspective as new relationships bloom. Children are a blessing at this time, keeping it real and helping us resist the adolescent urge to plunge headfirst into a new love that blots out all of the hurt from the failed marriage. Enjoy your children, take your time before beginning a new relationship, and wait before you involve your kids in that new romance."[33]

The following letter sent from the girlfriend of one of my clients to his ex-partner illustrates a more sensible approach toward dispelling anxieties regarding new partners:

Dear Amy,

We have yet to meet. I'd like to introduce myself. I am Susan Green. As you know, I have known Bob for eight months and we are involved in a committed relationship. Since our arrangement is not frivolous, and because your children and my children are connected by our relationship, I think it is important for us to meet.

I certainly am no authority on blended families, but I am aware of the emotional issues that children and ex-spouses can get caught up in. My intention is to ensure that the children's emotional needs are met and that problems are addressed with patience, a willingness to listen, and a positive approach to resolving them.

I believe strongly that blended families are successful when the relationship between the ex-spouses is one of cordiality, a commitment to mutual decision-making and one that focuses on the best interests of the children. I also believe that I must be willing to work co-operatively with you toward securing the children's best interests. I am willing to do that, Amy. I believe that is your intention as well. My son and your children's happiness and security are at stake.

I do hope, Amy, that you will accept my attempt to introduce myself. I want you to know that I am willing to co-operate with you in helping us find a way to ease the transition for our children. I do not mean to suggest we develop a social relationship; in fact, I don't believe that would be helpful. I would like the three of us to have an opportunity to discuss any relevant matters as soon as possible. Please feel free to arrange a time with Bob for that purpose, if it suits you.

I look forward to meeting with you.

Regards,
Susan

PARENTING PLANS

Before looking at a sample parenting plan in the Appendix, note that some couples come up with their own wording for a plan that works for their family. I wanted you to have an opportunity to look at two actual parenting plans that were authored by the couples themselves.

JILL AND SAM

Jill and Sam met and fell in love during college. They married soon after graduation and set about establishing themselves in their respective careers — he as a manager in a large computer software firm, she is a graphic designer. Over the next five years, they both became well-established in their respective careers, enabling them to maintain a comfortable lifestyle. In turn, that security was the basis on which they had two children, Andy and Sara, in quick succession.

Despite their heavy commitments to work, both were devoted and loving parents who shared this important task more or less equally. Over the next five years, however, their involvement in work and parenting took their toll. Both seemed to assume that that if their life was good in other respects, then surely their marriage would be good, as well. In fact, they gradually drifted apart, neither noticing the growing distance between them because their many other concerns absorbed all their time and energy. By the time they did notice, it was too late, both agreeing that perhaps it was best if they went their separate ways.

But that left them unclear about how to continue to provide the high-quality care they had always given to their children. Unable to conceive of not being involved in parenting on a regular basis, they were unable to work out an arrangement that pleased them both. They were preparing to fight it out in court when Jill's lawyer suggested family mediation.

Over the course of eight mediation sessions with me (three in pre-mediation), Jill and Sam were able to reach an agreement. The text of that document, minus the financial terms, is as follows:

Parenting Plan for Jill and Sam

We, Jill and Sam, have prepared the following draft Parenting Plan. In preparing this plan, we were guided by what we thought would be best for our children, Andy and Sara. We have devised a plan that will give them the opportunity to spend a substantial period of time with both parents with the least possible amount of disruption.

We, Jill and Sam, agree that we are both involved, committed, and loving parents who would like our children, Andy and Sara, to continue to have a meaningful relationship with each of us.

We have always shared in the responsibility of raising Andy and Sara and we continue to trust and respect each other as parents. We agree that our children will benefit from a positive relationship with each of us and are committed to a shared-parenting plan.

We agree that the children's primary residence will be with Jill and that they will spend time with Sam according to the following two-week schedule. During week one, Sam will pick up the children Thursday after school, keep them overnight, and return them to school Friday morning. He will also drive them to school on two mornings. During week two, Sam will pick up the children Thursday after school and they will live with him until he returns them to school Monday morning.

We agree that there shall be full disclosure between us in all matters concerning the welfare of Andy and Sara. We will confer as often as necessary to consider any matter requiring discussions, any problems or difficulties

We agree to discuss and make decisions together on all major issues relating to the children. Such issues shall include, but not be limited to, religious upbringing; education and choice of schools, health, and recreational activities; and attendance at any special events.

We agree that day-to-day decisions for the children will be the responsibility of the parent with whom they are residing, free of any interference from the other parent. We agree that although the parent with whom the children are residing has full responsibility in making day-to-day medical decisions, the other parent is to be involved in all major decisions and promptly consulted and advised about illnesses or accidents.

We agree that we will attempt to maintain consistency with respect to major household rules but will otherwise honour one another's parenting style, privacy, and authority. We agree not to interfere in the parenting style of the other parent nor will we make plans or arrangements that would impinge on the other parent's authority or times with the children without expressed agreement of the other parent. We agree to encourage Andy and Sara to discuss their grievances with a parent directly with the parent in question.

We agree that we shall each have two weeks during the summer holidays to spend with Andy and Sara, the exact dates to be discussed and agreed on between us. We will share time with the children on all other holidays according to a schedule to be discussed and agreed on between us. We agree that neither of us will move our permanent residence outside of the immediate jurisdiction.

We agree that we will work together to resolve any disputes that may arise in regard to the provisions of this agreement. If any disputes arise that we cannot resolve, we agree to enter mediation before seeking a solution in court.

JUDY AND ROBERT

The following couple was seen for five mediation sessions. They had a very positive relationship, probably owing to the fact that their separation was mutual in that they both felt they wanted to move on as they were unable to make their marriage work. Furthermore, they had been to marital counselling prior to the mediation.

Parenting Plan for Judy and Robert

General Philosophy: Since we believe in the importance of raising our children, we agree to share joint legal and physical custody of our children, Justin age 11 and Lisa age 10. We agree to be co-operative in the best interests of our children. Because we have difficulty settling on many issues, we agree to seek the help of a professional counsellor.

Co-operative parenting establishes a framework wherein, mutually or with a mediator, we agree to establish two homes for Justin and Lisa, arrange for the day-to-day care of Justin and Lisa, consult one another concerning the needs of the children and each other as their needs relate to Justin and Lisa. This framework does not require that any set methods of parenting be used but only that it be established in a co-operative manner.

Both of us understand that co-operative parenting requires the acceptance of mutual responsibilities as well as mutual rights insofar as Justin and Lisa are concerned and may require that we put both Justin and Lisa's needs ahead of our own. We set forth the following agreement as to the times and places where Justin and Lisa will reside, what our responsibilities will be, and other relevant factors. We further agree that this agreement will be reviewed at least on an annual basis and specifically renewed or revised as necessary.

We are aware that the court always has jurisdiction to modify any arrangement that concerns the well-being of Justin and Lisa. Notwithstanding this, we specifically express our intent to not resort to the court unless absolutely necessary.

While we were living together in a relationship, law and custom gave us certain rights and responsibilities regarding the parent-child interaction. It is our specific intent that these same rights and responsibilities continue, except as to those changes necessitated by the dissolution of our relationship and the establishment of two households. Since it was not necessary to be specific as to what the exact terms of the parent-child interactions were during our relationship, we do not feel that it is necessary to set forth all of the specific requirements of the new parent-child relationship. Such requirements as are set forth herein do not imply that this is a comprehensive or exclusive listing.

Both of us will continue to provide a home for Justin and Lisa until they reach adulthood. Each will care for the physical, emotional, and intellectual needs of our children as best we can; each will have the best interests of Justin and Lisa at heart.

We shall decide all issues, such as the time Justin and Lisa shall spend with us, schooling, medical care etc., between us, using the general intent of this agreement.

It is agreed that the parent with whom Justin and Lisa reside will have day-to-day jurisdiction of Justin and Lisa; however, all decisions of a substantive nature will be made by consensus, if time and circumstances reasonably permit.

Major decisions pertaining to the education, health, summer activities, and welfare of Justin and Lisa shall be decided by both of us after adequate consultation has occurred between us about the developmental stages of the children, the welfare of the children, the best interests of the children, and, so far as possible, the desires of the children.

Both of us agree to foster love and respect, even in trying times, between the children and the other parent. Neither of us shall do anything [that] may estrange Justin and Lisa from the other parent or hamper the natural and continuing relationships between the children and either parent.

We agree to honour one another's parenting style, privacy, and authority. We will not interfere in the parenting style of the other parent, nor will we make plans or arrangements that would impinge upon the other parent's authority or times with the children without the express agreement of the other parent.

Further, we understand that each of us has or may establish an emotional/romantic relationship with another adult and neither of us requires that such relationship be a marital relationship, nor shall either attempt to limit the parental rights of the other solely on the grounds that such a relationship is not a marital relationship.

The personal possessions of the children are, as we both acknowledge, their personal property. They are to have complete freedom as to where they want their personal property: they may leave clothing, shoes, etc., at either of their homes, subject to a reasonable rebalancing of those items at periodic intervals.

Parenting Schedule: Justin and Lisa will reside with Robert commencing at 5:00 p.m. on Sundays, Mondays, and Tuesdays. Judy will pick them up from school on Wednesday afternoon and they will reside with her on Wednesdays, Thursdays, and Fridays.

Every weekend will alternate between Judy and Robert.

Monday	Tuesday	Wednesday	Thursday	Friday	Saturday	Sunday
Robert picks up from school	Robert	Judy picks up from school	Judy	Alternate Friday evenings between Robert and Judy*	Judy or Robert on alternating weekends	Judy or Robert on alternating weekends**

* Whoever has the boys on the weekend has them from Friday evening onward. Robert will pick up from Judy at 7:00 p.m. on Friday when it is his weekend with the children.

** Judy will drop the children off at school Monday morning on her weekends with the children.

School breaks will be handled as follows:

- **Christmas Vacation:** The vacation will be divided in half, to include the use of a half-day if necessary. The shift between house-holds will occur at 12:00 noon on the appropriate day. Robert shall have the first half of Christmas vacation on even-numbered years, and July will have odd-numbered years.

Christmas Eve day and Christmas Day shall be handled as follows: Christmas Eve day, starting at 8:00 p.m. will be observed by the parent who has the children for the second half of the Christmas vacation. If Robert has the second half of the Christmas vacation, he will return the children to school on their first day back after the vacation, and Judy's parenting time will resume on that day.

- **Spring Break:** Spring break shall be alternated each year, with mother observing it with the children on even-numbered years, and Robert on odd-numbered years. Spring break will begin immediately after school on Friday. The parent who has them that year will pick up the children. The children will be returned to school by the spring break parent the following Monday.

- **Summer Vacation:** Summer vacation will be discussed in April. Barring any agreed changes, the current schedule will apply through the summer.

If away from home on vacation for more than a weekend, both parents are obligated to inform the other parent as to the destination, travel route, and flight information (if appropriate) at least ten days prior to the departure.

Holidays and birthdays will be handled as follows:

- **Mother's Day:** Regardless of their normal visitation schedule, the children will spend Mother's Day from 9:00 a.m. to 8:00 p.m. with Judy.

172

- **Father's Day:** Regardless of their normal visitation schedule, the children will spend Father's Day from 9:00 a.m. to 8:00 p.m. with Robert.

- **Thanksgiving Weekend:** The weekend will begin immediately after school on Wednesday and end with a return to school the following Monday. The weekend will alternate with spring break, so Judy will observe it with the children on even-numbered years and Robert on odd-numbered years.

- **New Year's Eve and Day:** The parent who has the children during the second half of the Christmas vacation will observe these days.

- **Easter Sunday:** Easter Sunday will be alternated each year, with Robert observing it with the children on odd-numbered years, and Judy on even-numbered years. It will begin at 6:00 p.m. Saturday night and end at 6:00 p.m. Sunday night.

- **Labour Day:** This weekend will begin immediately after school on Friday and end Tuesday morning when the children are returned to school. Robert will observe the weekend with the children on odd-numbered years and Judy on even-numbered years.

- **Father's and Mother's Birthdays:** Parent's birthdays will always transcend the regular visitation schedule. Since both parents' birthdays are during the school year, observation will begin immediately after school on school days and end at 8:00 p.m. On non-school days, the observation will begin at 9:00 a.m. and end at 8:00 p.m.

- ♦ **Children's Birthdays:** The children's birthdays will be observed with the parent with whom they reside when the birthday falls. The other parent will make alternative plans to celebrate the children's birthdays when the children are with him/her according to the normal co-parenting schedule.

Parental Contributions: We will both contribute a share of our resources (money, time, energy, effort, etc.) to the children for their material and psychological well-being. Each of us will provide the necessary food, clothing, medical and dental care, shelter, recreation, etc., as would be usual and reasonable for a person in his or her economic circumstances. Both of us shall provide medical and dental coverage when it is available through our employer.

Both of us agree to consult with one another concerning medical and dental insurance. We will determine which has the best plan for the best price and, if in agreement, obtain that plan. We agree to share the cost of that plan insofar as coverage for Justin and Lisa are concerned. We further agree to divide and pay any uncovered costs on a 50/50 basis where such charges are less than $100. When such charges exceed $100 and are of a non-emergency nature, we agree to consult and discuss such costs. We further agree to pay the charges that we do agree upon within thirty (30) days of submission.

Judy will provide her portion of the payment for daycare and schooling to Robert at least two business days before it is due and Robert will be responsible for making the actual payment.

Each child has a monthly education contribution of $100. Judy will pay Justin's education contribution and Robert will pay Lisa's education contribution.

Communication and Conflict Resolution: All communication about the children shall be written in a communication book, which shall pass with the children as they pass between households. In it are to be noted important events of the previous week, the children's health and need for current medication, and upcoming appointments that may affect the children's scheduling. Requests for adjustments in co-parenting times may also be entered. While each parent is encouraged to respond to all requests within 48 hours, silence in regard to a request shall be considered a "yes". The book may not be used to criticize either parent's behaviour.

Should any disputes arise between us or the children in the areas of education, health care, child care, religious training, operation of a motor vehicle, extra-curricular activities, vacations, or other significant issues, we agree that it is in the best interests of the children and ourselves to resolve any disputes. All such decisions must be made jointly or arbitrated; they may not be made unilaterally by either parent. Should either of us wish to modify this agreement, we agree to:

Meet and confer with one another, each to present to the other a proposed solution to the dispute. If there is no resolution at this step, we will then:

Meet and confer with an expert in the field related to the dispute, e.g., doctor, teacher, counsellor, etc. If there is no resolution at this step, we will then:

Meet and confer with a mediator/counsellor who has had experience in dispute resolution. All concerned shall use their best efforts to resolve the issues. Should there be no resolution at this step then we will submit the matter to a court of competent jurisdiction. We understand that this is an extraordinary step and will be resorted to only when there is no other way to resolve the problem.

This section shall apply to all parts of this agreement:

Until there is resolution of any dispute that may arise concerning this agreement, the operative terms of this agreement shall remain in full force and effect.

Miscellaneous

- **Child Illnesses:** If a child is too ill to go to school (or camp in the summer), then a parent must stay home with the sick child. On Mondays and Tuesdays, that parent will be Robert. On Thursdays and Fridays, that parent will be Judy. On Wednesdays, it will be whichever parent is more available, and in the case of a dispute, it will be the parent that has the children for the upcoming weekend. Obviously, both parents are to inform the other of routine illnesses [that] require the child to stay home from school.
- **Out of Town Travel:** If a parent travels out of town for fewer than 48 hours, that parent is responsible for arranging childcare for the children. If a parent is going to be gone for more than 48 hours, then the other parent must be offered first right of refusal. If that parent cannot care for the children, it is up to the travelling parent to

176

arrange full-time childcare until the return. If a parent accepts care of the children, there will be no makeup time for the absent parent.

- **Telephone Access:** The children may call the other parent whenever they like. Each parent may call the children once per every 24 hours of absence. The children are to be given privacy for their telephone conversations by the other parent.
- **Transportation:** The basic principle is that the parent having the child is responsible to deliver the child either to the other parent who is supposed to have the child, or to the event or activity the child is expected to attend.
- **Day-to-Day Decisions:** Decisions about bedtime, hygiene, minor disciplinary actions, minor medical and dental procedures, curfew, chores, allowances, social dress, and jewellery shall be the province of the household in which the child dwells at the moment.
- **Emergencies:** Each parent is required to notify the other parent immediately of any medical emergency. The parent present is authorized to sign legal consents for both parents to permit emergency intervention.
- **Information:** Each parent is required to set up his/her own information network for information about school and routine medical appointments. Each is required to tell professionals that they hold joint custody and each parent has equal rights to access all information. On any emergency information sheet, each parent will list the other as the first person to contact if he or she is not reachable.
- **Geographical Relocation:** Relocation within 20 miles may be done only after Mediation/Arbitration

has taken place as to the required changes in the children's schooling, daycare, and after-school activities. The children may not be removed permanently from their respective location without the express approval of the other parent, a Mediation/Arbitration decision, or an order of the court.

• **Review and Agreement:** During the months of April each year, Judy and Robert will review these custody arrangements and address any issues that have arisen. This will be done at the same time that summer vacations are discussed. If both parties agree, these arrangements may be reviewed at any other time during the year.

In another mediation situation, I worked with the parents of a seven-year-old boy who sent me the following email. They wanted it included in their parenting plan — clearly a thoughtful and helpful understanding for what was best for their son. I think, whenever possible, it is much better for parents to work together and design their own unique plan. Having the authorship of the plan will make it easier for them to commit to and follow the plan as they designed it.

We strongly believe that Joe should have a loving, safe, fun, and secure relationship with both his mother and father, notwithstanding the fact that we will be living in separate homes.

We want Joe to feel equally at ease in both homes without having to worry about his parents not being together.

We want Joe to have stability and reinforcement that despite our separation that we are his parents for life. We want Joe to be close to both of us, respect each of us, and be able to count on both of us for support and guidance.

As Joe's parents, we should support Joe and promote a positive relationship with the other parent.

We want Joe to be clear about the arrangements for spending time with each parent. Joe should not be exposed to sudden changes in arrangements unless it is unavoidable.

Joe should not be exposed to continuing conflict as it is harmful to him.

We should be committed to taking into account Joe's feelings about the arrangements we make at all times.

Joe will do best when both of us have a stable and meaningful involvement in Joe's life. Each of us have different and valuable contributions to make to Joe's development, and as parents we must recognize our differences.

We should help Joe to maintain positive existing relationship with school friends and kids where he lives, routines and activities.

Communication and co-operation between us is very important when arranging Joe's activities.

As parents we should refrain from any form of reliance on Joe to communicate information between us.

As parents we should respect the privacy of the other parent and refrain from engaging Joe in any discussion or questioning about the other parent's personal life or activities.

Consistent rules and values in both households will create a sense of security for Joe and will ensure he grows up with a strong sense of values and commitment.

We as his parents should allow Joe to bring personal items back and forth between homes, no matter who purchased them.

Our parenting plan should be adjusted over time as our family's needs, schedules, and circumstances change.

Joe's social activities and commitments should be given priority. We as his parents need to support Joe's participation in his activities.

8

Don't Be Derailed
by Financial Issues

Don't get even, get equal.

You now have a very good grasp of shared-parenting plans. This chapter serves to help you understand the financial issues that arise from divorce and new parenting arrangements. Understanding these issues will help you keep them from derailing your parenting plan. Each jurisdiction has different financial laws. I have kept this discussion general to get at the financial principles involved.

Parenting and financial issues are inextricably linked, with decisions in one necessarily affecting decisions in the other. For example, parenting involves decisions not only about time-sharing and decision-making, but also about child-care costs, future plans, and how these costs will be shared.

A comprehensive approach will maximize your self-determination. No one knows your children better than you do. You should be the ones who decide what is best for them. The same is true regarding finances and necessary financial decisions that arise from your divorce.

Parenting and money involve different orders of experience. Parenting tends to be immediate and emotionally charged. Money tends to be removed, factual, and heavily symbolic, as in lines of credit and interest-bearing investments. However, it can also be emotionally charged, and that will depend on a variety of factors.

In general, even at the outset, financial mediation will require that you engage with a mediator and or a lawyer with both clinical and technical skill sets. The particular balance between the two will vary as your situation unfolds. In my experience, clinical skills are especially helpful in the beginning phases of your divorce, while technical skills become increasingly important toward the middle and end phases.

Financial mediation will centre on three important areas: child support, spousal maintenances, and property division, with tax implications a concern throughout.

Given this, I recommend that you engage in co-mediation with a clinically trained family mediator and a financially trained family mediator. Or you may want to engage a comprehensive family mediator who has the training required to do both. It's also a good idea for you to have your family lawyers involved, especially in the financial aspects, to make sure that there has been honest disclosure and that all aspects required under the law have been fully met.

The remainder of this chapter discusses the relational/financial issues that are inextricably bound up in your divorce, which may have an impact not only on you, but on your children as well. The details regarding many financial issues are related to the actual laws in your particular jurisdiction.

In both the United States and Canada, the assumption of shared responsibility for child care extends to sharing the burden of its costs. The details regarding the financial aspects are quite comprehensive and require lengthy exploration. This chapter deals only with how relational concerns impact the financial aspects and vice versa.

Following are the four main financial/relational family patterns that crop up during mediation:

Pattern 1: Money as Power

Some husbands believe that the money belongs to them. They are both offended and confused by notions of "community property." This view is likely reflected in a fairly clean division of family roles, with work and finances in the husband's/ father's realm, and family and emotional matters, including child care, household management, education, and health care, in the wife's/mother's realm.

In this arrangement, husbands typically give their wives a regular household "allowance" but maintain control of the remainder. In divorce, such a husband feels that he, and he alone, should decide how the money should be divided and, conversely, that any claims that his spouse might make lack all credibility.

Occasionally this may be the case. For example, some wives may have no knowledge of what their husbands earn, whether there are savings and how much has been saved, or whether there are any investments. They may also have little or no knowledge of the tax system or the valuation of pensions, investments, or the matrimonial home. They may feel overwhelmed by the entire process of negotiating financial matters.

Such husbands and wives approach mediation in very different terms. Husbands are often contemptuous of their wife's lack of knowledge about money, deny that they had any role in maintaining their wife's lack of financial knowledge, and are often very angry that state or provincial statutes force them to share assets that they feel belong to them. In contrast, wives often report a long and ultimately futile struggle to achieve a more balanced relationship. Such women are apt

183

to approach mediation with a combination of anger, intimidation, and helplessness.

Ironically, there are often two elephants in the room. The husband's unexpressed concern is whether he will get to see his kids for significant enough amounts of time and whether he can afford the divorce, given the support payments he will be expected to pay. Meanwhile, the wife's unaddressed concern is what might happen when the kids are with the husband, and whether he will pay adequate support.

If financial conflicts or impasses are involved in your case, your mediator may have to work with you at the relational level in terms of power balancing, confrontation, education, and role reversal. Your mediator may meet with you and your spouse individually. For you to protect your children, both of you must allow your mediator to help the "money manager" to relinquish some control and the "money innocent" to take some control.

A mediator may also need to confront a husband's distorted beliefs, for example, that the money belongs to him and that the wife has contributed little of value, that the wife's lack of knowledge about money is irremediable, or that financial mediation merely involves a good business plan devoid of affect.

A mediator may also need to confront a wife's distorted beliefs, for example, that the husband cares only about the money, that a husband's control over the family's resources represents a character flaw, that negotiating with him is futile, or that the organization of their roles in the family was a personal choice and thus independent of any larger forces in society.

If you are in this situation, your mediator may work with you together and separately to achieve a balance from which you can negotiate an agreement and plan for your children. In my experience, as parents hear each other more clearly through this process, the money manager is able to relinquish some control and the money innocent to gain some control. Note that as in all cases involving financial mediation, spouses will routinely be asked to consult with their lawyers to ensure that any agreement between them is fair and reasonable.

Consider the story of Mark and Dorothy Gentle.

Dorothy was raised in a secure, middle-class family. Her father had always been in charge of the family's resources, so she was not surprised when Mark did the same when they married. Mark had come from a working-class family where every dollar counted and where both parents shared in financial decision-making. He was both surprised and flattered to find himself in charge of the money when he married.

Because they had little money to speak of at the time — Dorothy had married for love and against parental resistance — that control was easy to assume. His later success as an entrepreneur changed everything, leaving him in charge of a comfortable income, mounting debts, and an unwillingness to share information about either with Dorothy.

Instead, he spent lavishly on his wife and his three children. But the time he needed to generate that income — time away from his family — eroded his marriage, and his refusal to share control over the money with Dorothy eroded it further. When she had a rather public affair with a younger (and much poorer) man, even marital counselling could not save their relationship; it was all over for both of them.

In mediation, the Gentles were cordial and mutually respectful as they created a parenting plan. But when the discussion turned to money, they were transformed into a high-conflict couple who raged at each other through tears.

Their initial conversation was loud, filled with mutual accusations and name-calling, and quite unproductive. Furthermore, with his background in business, Mark was completely contemptuous of the size of Dorothy's claim for property division and alimony.

Individual discussions with Dorothy revealed that she felt overwhelmed and quite unprepared to negotiate the money issues. Subsequent efforts to educate her, control their emotional outbursts, give each a glimpse of what the other was experiencing, and create a level playing field proved lengthy but ultimately successful.

Their hard-fought final agreement was not only mutually acceptable but was based on a newfound mutual respect and some new skills in conflict management. Both lawyers confirmed that the deal they reached was a reasonable one.

Pattern 2: Money as Security

The tremendous influx of women into the workplace has created "hybrid couples" who combine elements of the new with elements of the traditional.

They are a new couple in that both work, contribute to their combined family income, and so share in financial decision-making. However, they are often traditional in at least two senses: wives remain largely responsible for child care, and the organization of the workplace means that they often earn less — sometimes much less — than their husbands.

Their income may give these wives options that their mothers did not enjoy, but many of them are still in a position of financial dependence. Among families with children, a wife's income may be dedicated to their needs, whereas all other expenses are paid for out of their husband's income.

Divorce, then, can create a dilemma and in some cases may even push these wives and their children into poverty. Among those in long-term marriages, whose children are often grown and no longer living with them, divorce confronts these wives with the bleak prospect of facing retirement alone and with very limited resources.

For pattern two couples, financial mediation focuses on the issue of financial security.

In my experience, there is often a hysterical edge to negotiation in these cases, as husbands and wives talk at cross-purposes. Husbands tend to use the language of business: fact-based, unemotional, and centred on creating a sound business plan. In contrast, wives tend to use the language of hurt feelings. They complain that husbands have not listened to their concerns and still continue not to do so. They insist that mediation must give them what they deserve for years of devotion.

Your mediator may suggest individual meetings because you are talking past each other in joint sessions. Once each of you understands both your financial tendencies and concerns, you can be brought back together for negotiation.

On the other hand, joint sessions in which you reverse role-play help some couples to really hear what the other is saying. Public disclosure of family resources is also vital to ensure that both of you negotiate with real numbers.

Consider the story of Sam and Maria Papas. Sam and Maria met during their last year in high school. They were attracted to each other because both were of Greek extraction, had had virtually no dating experience, and thought the other "nice."

Sam and Maria continued to date until both graduated from university, when they married. However, within a few months of their marriage, both realized that they were dramatically incompatible in a variety of ways. Divorce was not an option, however, as both were devout Eastern Orthodox Christians. Through tacit agreement, they simply carried on. Thirty years later, when their last child left for university, they finally decided to get divorced.

Throughout their time together, Sam had been continuously employed in the computer industry. In contrast, Maria, although qualified in education, had stayed home with the children until they entered primary school. Consequently, although Sam was well prepared financially for retirement, Maria was not. Moreover, their efforts to negotiate money issues were blocked by a very destructive conflict style in which issues were seldom, if ever, resolved.

I used role reversal role-playing to help each of them gain insight into the other's concerns and fears. I also took them through training in conflict and communication skills, which allowed them to negotiate issues to resolution for the first time.

The process was so successful that Sam and Maria briefly toyed with the idea of reconciliation. In the end, however, both decided to carry on with the divorce. In addition, once Sam realized that he could keep his pension and trade off for other assets, he made Maria a fair financial offer that she accepted, after conferring with her lawyer. They also agreed to put aside some money to ensure that their youngest child would complete university.

Pattern 3: Money as Painkiller/Revenge

Just as marriages vary in how they begin, so they vary in how they end. Three common routes to divorce are:

* the unilateral or mutual loss of interest;
* the build-up of frustration and misunderstanding, leading to chronic conflict; and
* the build-up of frustration and anger, culminating in some sort of traumatic event, such as a violent episode or, more typically, infidelity.

For the last two variations, money can be one path to redemption by acting as a painkiller and/or as the basis on which one spouse seeks to get revenge on the other. In this pattern, the "injured" spouse will typically make exaggerated claims for property division, based on his or her pain rather than any real numbers. In some cases, one party may manipulate the numbers to his or her own end.

For example, in a recent case, a husband abandoned his wife of twenty-seven years for a woman fourteen years his junior. In revenge, his wife spent or liquidated more than half a million dollars in assets so that she could claim a large alimony award. In other cases in which I have been involved, property may be damaged or sold, spouses may become obsessed with money matters, or apartments or houses may be broken into.

In short, Pattern 3 situations can bring out the worst in people and can engage them in behaviour that is absolutely out of keeping with their normal conduct. As the typical injured party, a wife's emotional tone varies between unbridled rage, intense pain, great bitterness, and, underneath it all, deep sadness. By contrast, a husband's emotional tone varies between contempt, anger, guilt, and confusion.

Both may attempt to recruit the children to their side and in front of them may paint the other parent in the blackest possible terms. In turn, in the vice of a loyalty bind, the children may show various signs of distress and/or alienation. The spouses may be unaware of their children's distress or may lay blame squarely on the shoulders of the other parent, thus denying their own role in this process.

Under these chaotic conditions, families fall into two groups:

1. Those who are committed to "winning" in litigation will be uninterested in mediation and may stonewall any such suggestions by judges, lawyers, or the other spouse. Such couples would likely make very poor candidates for mediation in any event because they typically advance entrenched and often frankly irrational beliefs about the other spouse and, at this point, are prepared to risk everything they own or can borrow to "win."

2. Those who have at least some awareness of what this process is doing to their children and can be persuaded, either by a lawyer and/or a parent, to try mediation.

189

In mediation, such couples present as emotionally unstable, impulsive, and very difficult to control. They are often more interested in expressing their feelings than engaging in productive negotiation, and the underlying trauma may or may not be mentioned explicitly. However, in individual sessions they do recognize that what is happening between them has been harmful to their children. They often turn to the mediator to help them stop their emotional outbursts when they themselves cannot; temporarily, they may need external controls when their internal controls have been overwhelmed by their feelings.

Mediators often take three steps to help Pattern 3 couples:

1. The first step involves putting a heavy-handed, even authoritarian, emphasis on the rules of conduct in mediation. This is coupled with the repeated emphasis on the best interests of the children as the key motive for staying in mediation. In this way the mediator establishes external limits and controls, which is the only way such couples can learn to interact productively.

2. The second step involves addressing the sources of their respective anger. The mediator may suggest moving between joint and individual sessions, role reversal, and the public airing of family secrets. In some cases, the construction of a forgiveness ritual in which pain, guilt, and forgiveness play central roles can be helpful. Involving the children directly can also be helpful, because the mediator can gain permission from them to say what they themselves cannot say to their parents.

3. The third step, which can overlap the second, involves addressing the substantive issues that brought the couple to mediation in the first place. This is often a slow process but, given tight control

and dogged determination on the part of the mediator, can move these couples ahead to the point where a full agreement is possible.

Consider, for example, the case of Adam and Maria Quinn.

The Quinns came from very different backgrounds. Maria came from a large, volatile, but loving Italian family. She was not at all put off by loud conflict and was herself prone to angry outbursts. But these outbursts were short-lived and followed by displays of affection.

In contrast, Adam was the only child of a rigidly controlled British family in which open displays of feelings were forbidden. Thus, opposites attracted, for their initial relationship was intense and passionate.

Over time, however, these differences took their toll, with Adam preferring to escape the conflict rather than confront it. He had his first brief "fling," as he put it, after eight years of marriage. Over the next ten years, six more affairs occurred, all brief and secret from Maria. It was a casual relationship that turned serious that finally led to their separation.

In mediation, initial efforts at negotiation proved futile. Maria's anger would quickly boil over into furious attacks on Adam. Adam responded by alternating between becoming cold and distant or guilty and apologetic. In either case, productive negotiation was impossible.

To get the couple on track, rigid rules of respectful conduct were laid down and scrupulously enforced. Although outwardly they displayed dwindling resistance, they seemed relieved. The intensity of their feelings was such that self-control had been impossible. Moving between joint and individual sessions, as well as using role reversal and communication exercises, gave them the opportunity to talk out their feelings and gain some understanding that both were going through a very difficult time.

Maria focused on her sense of betrayal, failure, and loss and Adam expressed his guilt, anger, and bitterness. Both were reluctantly able to acknowledge that Maria's tendency to attack and Adam's tendency to withdraw were poor ways of handling conflict. This allowed Maria to accept Adam's apology, although it did not diminish either one's pain. But both were able to go on to negotiate their substantive issues, though maintaining this focus proved difficult.

Both were able to monitor the intensity of their emotions when they realized the consequences to their children if they failed in mediation. In the end, they did agree on all issues in dispute, with the agreement sent on to their respective lawyers for detailed review.

Pattern 4: Money as Closure

As noted earlier in this chapter, some marriages end in anger and conflict, whereas others close in silence and chronic fatigue. The latter characterizes pattern 4 couples. There are no fireworks here, only depressed resignation. These couples come in for mediation showing low energy and describing vague concerns, mostly centred on anxious uncertainty about the future. Thus, their primary concern is to bring matters to a close as soon as possible, but they are unclear as to the technical matters involved in doing so.

Token conflict can occur over assets of sentimental value, but otherwise such couples are in general agreement about asset valuation and division. Assured of equity in asset division, money is often not an important issue. In this context, the mediator has three things to offer such couples.

First, they offer a clear and structured process for addressing all substantive issues. Having someone who knows what he or she is doing and can walk them through the process greatly assists such couples and dramatically reduces their anxiety. It often raises a series of financial issues neither would have thought of if left to their own devices.

Second, they provide good technical knowledge. Spouses need the right information on which to make informed choices. In the case of couples with many assets, the involvement of their respective lawyers and/or accountants can be very important.

And third, they give emotional support. Given their sadness, these spouses may not have the energy to make the decisions they need to make, or they may act impulsively, without thinking through the consequences of one or another choice. They may retreat from decision-making in confusion or uncertainty and may have difficulty staying focused. This support supplies them with the energy they need to continue, provides them with a context in which to explore their sense of mutual failure, and gives them the hope of full and final closure, so that they can each move on with their lives.

Consider the story of David and Ann Samson. Both had married late in recognition of their educational and professional objectives — he as an economist, she as a financial planner. Both soon discovered, however, that their real commitment was to their respective careers and not to each other.

Five years into their marriage, with two children now, they decided to end their marriage by mutual consent. Although both were very well informed about finances, they had little knowledge about asset division in divorce. That uncertainty, coupled with their depression and anxiety, led them to mediation.

Mediation with this couple was centred more on support than on negotiation. In fact, once the various components of financial mediation were explained to them, consensus based on equity was relatively easy to achieve. Indeed, more time was spent exploring their feelings and helping them achieve a sense of closure on their relationship than discussing money.

With the completion of their agreement, separation counselling was recommended to help them understand why their marriage had failed and to move on with their respective lives, thus enabling them to focus on their children's needs.

Keeping in mind that protecting your children is job number one, you are well advised to guard against being derailed by money issues. Money issues almost always come clothed in relational issues, and vice versa. Mediation allows you to stay in charge of these important concerns, instead of taking your conflict to court and letting someone else take charge of them.

Conclusion

What we will call the beginning is often the
end and to make an end is to make a begin-
ning. The end is where we start from.
— T.S. Eliot

We in Western societies are far enough along in the "age of divorce" to be able to see what works and what doesn't for children and families when marriages come to an end.

We know for a fact that when divorce agreements are hammered out in court, they involve competitiveness, territorialism, aggression, and an intense and compulsive desire to win, and they result in long-term pain for all involved.

We also know that, by contrast, when divorce agreements and parenting plans are developed through divorce mediation, the emotional and financial costs of divorce are decreased by building on the parents' constructive co-operation for the sake of their children.

No one truly wins when a marriage comes apart, whether the divorce is handled by the adversary system or the mediation system. However, through mediation, instead of both spouses losing because their kids lose, all parties benefit because they are working together for the family's ongoing health.

When I started to develop the theoretical foundations of therapeutic family mediation in 1980, I hoped that before long the approach would be considered the first choice in divorce cases. That day has not yet come; however, the legal system and society are increasingly "getting it." They are becoming aware that resources should be made available to families when divorce enters their lives to prevent further fallout through court battles. Mediation, co-mediation, collaborative law, alternative dispute resolutions — these new legal methods are being enacted by lawyers, mediators, counsellors, and social workers to help families make a new beginning based on hope instead of on regret, resentment, and anger.

I believe we are getting closer to a time when the fear engendered by adversary divorce will be eliminated, a time when decisions to break up or stay together are made for the right reasons — the health, safety, growth, and happiness of family members.

That hope is partly based on the results of research studies carried out over the past several years. In my own research conducted at the family court in Toronto, we interviewed more than four hundred families who participated in two research studies.

Approximately 70 percent of the families who were referred for mediation reached an agreement without going to trial. The majority of these cases were custody and/or access disputes. Furthermore, a follow-up interview some three to four months later revealed that 80 percent of those who had reached an agreement had either fully or partially maintained the original agreement.

A second follow-up of the court records one year later, although not complete, showed that the initial trend of 80 percent appeared to be holding. Referrals from lawyers that are made early in the legal process seem to have a higher rate of agreement than those referred directly from the judge at the time of the hearing.

Another important finding is that the majority of cases in mediation reach agreement with fewer than six interviews. The model of short-term counselling seems to be most effective. The majority of the clients (70 percent) reported that things had changed for the better and that they had benefited substantially from the service.

In a related study that I have also conducted, fifty-three lawyers were interviewed following their involvement with the mediation service. Approximately 80 percent were in favour of the service and said they would recommend the service to other lawyers. The overwhelming majority of lawyers felt that the mediation service is valuable in that it:

1. Helps avoid unnecessary litigation.
2. Better prepares the parties to understand the issues.
3. Allows the client to use legal services more appropriately.
4. Reduces the clients' emotional turmoil.

Contested divorce in all its guises will always be with us and will be used by those couples who are unable or unwilling to dissolve their marriages in any other manner. These are marriages whose rational dissolution is impossible — marriages that will end in the traditional way with custody being awarded in the traditional way.

Family mediation has become extremely popular in North America and in other industrialized countries around the world. Partially, this is so for practical reasons. Divorce rates remain high, and approximately half of the people married today will be divorced in the future. Court dockets remain correspondingly clogged. Mediation provides an effective means of court diversion. That said, family mediation is not a static approach. Rather, it continues to evolve and change, grow and develop.

In a recent report from the Ontario Law Commission regarding the family law system, it was stated that the current system bankrupts litigants and routinely fails to deal with the wishes and concerns of children. "Children want to be heard but they feel they have no voice and no power in relation to adults, including their parents, lawyers, councillors and judges."[34]

However, our goal should be to make the system in which one party is pitted against the other the method of last resort. This would constitute a major revolution. I hope that this book has persuaded you, if you are headed for or involved in a divorce, to join this revolution.

Do it for the sake of your children.

Appendix

The following is an actual parenting plan (only the names have been changed). This plan is much more structured than the two in Chapter 7, the reason being that Joan and Tom Smith wanted it that way because they had difficulties communicating properly and wanted to have a default mechanism in their plan. Yours will vary in many points, but this gives you a good feel for creating your own plan.

MEMORANDUM OF UNDERSTANDING BETWEEN:

Joan Smith
and
Tom Smith

Parental Guidelines

1. Children of divorce do best in the short- and long-run when they feel loved and cared for by both parents. This is most likely to occur when the children have ongoing contact with

both parents who participate fully in their lives. Children feel more secure and better about themselves knowing both parents want them and want to be involved in their lives, and it helps diminish feelings of abandonment and rejection. Children also need consistency and stability. The children's need for frequent contact and for stability must be adjusted to arrive at a healthy balance. This balance will depend on many factors, including those related to the children (e.g., their ages, developmental needs, and temperaments), the parents, and the circumstances.

2. Most children in divorced families struggle to some extent with a loyalty bind, that is, they feel torn when their commitment to one parent may be seen as disloyalty to the other parent. How this manifests is related to many factors, including the children's age, their developmental levels, their temperament, and their academic, social, and emotional adjustment.

    Parental behaviour is a major factor, as well. Thus a parent can do many things to minimize the effects of the loyalty bind and to promote the children's positive adjustment. Some of the things parents can do are explained below.

    Healthy child adjustment requires each parent's implicit and explicit permission and acceptance for the children to have a relationship with the other parent. The parents should acknowledge to the children the relevance of the other parent to the child's lives.

    The children's overall adjustment and their relationship with both parents will be compromised if they are exposed to disapproving attitudes or negative comments about the other parent; and/or if one parent undermines the other (even when he or she thinks the other parent deserves it). This applies when the children may be in the vicinity, playing in the other room or "probably asleep." Parents should not allow any other person to denigrate the other parent in front of the children. Parents are advised to refer to any differences between homes as "differences," and not it terms of one being "better" or "worse" than the other.

The children have been exposed to such denigration when one parent blames the other for the divorce, or undermines the other with derogatory comments, or is critical of the other's lifestyle or personality. When this occurs, the children will have difficulty showing that he or she is happy spending time with the other parent, as this would only let their present parent down. In an effort to cope, the children may say things to each parent he or she thinks they want or need to hear. These comments may be distortions, exaggerations, or even untruths said to appease or ingratiate themselves to their parents, such as not enjoying an outing, having only eaten junk food, having stayed up very late, and other misrepresentations or exaggerations of what a parent said or did. Such behaviour on the part of the children is very common.

If one parent finds that what the children have said is of significant concern, that parent should first ask the other parent what actually happened in a non-judgmental way. Also, children who are repeatedly caught in a loyalty bind become masters of manipulation, for example, by learning to play one parent off against the other. Often, the result is that the children lose respect for both parents. If a complaint is made to one parent about the other, the children should be encouraged to talk directly to the parent he or she is complaining about.

Further, each parent should respect the other's privacy and not ask the children questions about the other parent's personal life or activities. Rather, showing a casual interest in the children's activities is important for the children's self-esteem. At the same time, the parents are wise to recognize the difference between open-ended casual questions of interest and pointed and repeated questioning.

Casual questioning would include questions such as, "How are you?", "How did you enjoy your time?", or "What did you do that was fun?" as well as picking up on the children's spontaneous statements. In contrast, pointed questioning would include questions such as, "Where did you go?", "Who was that?", or "How long did you stay?" Although the parent may be genuinely interested, pointed questions tend to put undue pressure on the children, and may negatively affect their adjustment.

3. The negative effect on inter-parental conflict on child adjustment has been well-documented. "Every missile we send to our ex-spouse goes through the heart of our child(ren)." In addition to providing a poor and negative model, observing parents verbally mistreat one another communicates to the children that their parents do not mutually respect or like each other. In turn, this message exacerbates the children's loyalty bind and negatively affects all aspects of their adjustment. Healthy child adjustment requires parental co-operation, mutual respect, and the absence of inter-parental conflict. Any discussions between the parents at transitions times must be limited to brief and cordial exchanges. The parents are wise to work toward establishing a "business" relationship with each other for the sake of the children.

Regular meetings and/or telephone calls should be arranged. If these are impossible or ineffective, the parents need to communicate in writing or through a third party. Financial matters should not be discussed in front of the children. Co-operative parenting is best for healthy child adjustment. If the parents cannot remain amicable, it is better for them to remain disengaged than to expose the children to conflict.

4. It will damage the children's current and future adjustment if he or she is relied upon to carry messages (including

support cheques) between the parents. It is imperative that the parents not rely on the children for communication. If the children ask either parent for a change in the time-sharing schedule, the parent is advised to say that the parents will discuss the matter, decide if they can accommodate the request, and get back to the children.

5. Difficulties with transitions and with "settling back down" after time with the other parent are to be expected. While these adjustments are due, in part, to the children's exposure to different routines and different child management styles, difficulties at transition times have less to do with the children's experience of the other parent and more to do with the transition itself and with their parent's conduct. Parents are advised to examine their role in the children's difficulties with transitions and with "settling in." If one parent undermines the other, even covertly, as described above, the children may show disrespect for and test the limits with the undermined parent. These parent-child conflicts (which to some extent are normal) will influence the children's ability to resettle into the routines upon re-entering the undermined parent's home. Most children will come to adjust to differences in routines and lifestyles between their parents. The parent's sensitivity to the children's predicament and loyalty bind is critical at transition times. Coming down hard on children to quickly resume usual routines is unlikely to be as effective as a combination of empathy, flexibility, and firmness.

Parenting Plan

Introduction: Joan and Tom shall share responsibility for their two children, Brenda, age 9 and David, age 7. In spite of the usual and holiday schedule, child-related decision-making, and dispute resolution methods shall be as per the following parenting plan.

The parents are committed to the spirit of the parenting plan, which recognizes the children's need for a good and ongoing relationship with both parents, and which calls for shared responsibility, with both parents involved in all matters related to the children.

Sharing responsibility for parenting involves two major aspects: (1) how major child-related decisions are made; and (2) the time the children spend with both parents. The primary goals are to minimize factors that produce or promote interparental conflict, to ensure smooth implementation of the parenting plan, and to maximize healthy child adjustment. The decisions that typically and most frequently challenge families are those related to day-to-day family management. These include: parental values and morals; clothes and toys travelling back and forth; parent-child telephone contact; transportation between homes; discipline, consistency, and routines; changes and flexibility; extracurricular activities; parental communication; holiday schedules; parenting approaches; and exchanges of information.

Sharing responsibilities poses a challenge for most families, as ineffective communication, mutual animosity, and power and control issues contribute to impasses. To the extent that it minimizes factors that produce conflict, a structured and specific parenting plan is preferred. Such plans provide solutions to day-to-day family management dilemmas and a method for making child-related decisions.

All possible changes in family circumstances and management cannot, of course, be foreseen no matter how comprehensive or thorough the plan. Children mature and change, as do their needs. Parents may move residence or change employment, remarry or divorce, thus encountering new living arrangements and new family dynamics. Any parenting plan will therefore require revision over time.

Appendix

In the interest of clarity, when the children are with their father, he will be referred to as the "resident" parent, and when the children are with their mother, she will be referred to as the "resident" parent.

A. Child-Related Decision-Making

1. Health Care

a. Routine of Daily Health Care:

    i. The parents shall continue to use the services of Dr. ____ as the children's family doctor, Dr. ____ as the children's dentist, and Dr. ____ as the children's paediatrician.

    ii. The parents will provide each other with the names, addresses, and telephone numbers of all physicians, dentists, orthodontists, or other professionals providing care to the children.

    iii. The resident parent is responsible for making day-to-day medical decisions (such as giving over-the-counter medicines, keeping the children home from school due to illness, taking the children to see a doctor for minor illnesses, etc.).

    iv. The children shall not be expected to travel between homes if, in the judgment of the resident parent, they are too ill to do so. The other parent will accept this judgment and will not expect any makeup time.

    v. The children shall not be expected to travel between homes if, in the judgment of the other parent, they themselves are too ill to receive them. The resident parent will accept this judgment and the other parent will not expect any makeup time.

205

vi. Both parents will have equal access to the children's health cards.

b. Major Medical Decisions (including long-term medication/treatment, surgery, orthodontic work, etc.)

    i. The parents shall notify each other of a child's or children's emergency visit to a physician, specialist, and/or hospital. Both parents may attend.

    ii. Each parent shall provide written permission to the children's physicians to release information to the other parent.

    iii. The parents shall directly request any relevant records/information from the children's physicians and not expect the other parent to provide such records or updates.

    iv. Major medical decisions are usually infrequent. However, because they are serious, it is in the children's best interest for both parents to be involved in major medical decisions, with the assistance of expert third parties, such as medical specialists, dentists, and so on. The parents will notify each other of any potential major medical decisions as well as provide the others with the name(s) and telephone number(s) of the attending physician(s). It is ideal for the parents to consult with the physician(s) together. However, if this is not possible, the parents may consult individually, adding second opinions as they think necessary. The parents shall arrive at major medical decisions mutually. If they cannot, they shall abide by the consensus medical opinion, in consultation with Dr. Howard Irving, as outlined in paragraph 12 of this section (Dispute Resolution Mechanism).

2. **Education** (Including school and nanny selection, psycho educational testing, remedial assistance, report cards, parent-teacher meetings, etc.)

    i.   It is in the children's best interest if the parents attend parent-teacher meetings together. In doing so, the children will perceive that their parents are working together on their behalf. This may lessen the children's loyalty bind and curtail any effort on their part to "play both ends against the middle." If either parent prefers to have an individual meeting, each parent will be responsible for arranging with the school his or her own parent-teacher meeting. Any special meetings, involving board or school personnel (other than the teacher), are likely to require the parents to attend together, as time and resources usually do not allow for separate meetings.

    ii. Each parent will be responsible for staying up to date on any relevant educational matters and requesting involvement for any special meetings about their children. Each parent will request from the school that he or she is provided with all notices, report cards, progress reports, and so on. If the school cannot accommodate such requests, each parent will continue to notify the other of all school events at the time he or she learns of them. The residential parent who first obtains the children's report cards or progress reports will provide the other parent with copies of them.

    iii. It is in the children's best interests for both parents to attend school-related functions, such as open houses, plays, concerts, fundraisers, and so on. The children's relatives are welcome to attend as desired.

    iv. Major decisions related to the children's education including class placement, psycho educational testing, remedial assistance, enrichment, and so on shall be made by both parents. Such decisions will be made in consultation with relevant experts, including teachers, principals, school or independent psychologists, and so on. It is ideal for the parents to consult with these professionals together. However, if this is not possible, the parents may consult individually, adding second opinions as necessary. The parents will make educationally relevant decisions mutually, in consultation with the relevant expert or experts, if there are different expert opinions. If the parents cannot agree, they will follow the "Dispute Resolution Mechanism" outlined in paragraph 11.

v. The school will have both parents' names to call in case of an emergency. The parents will be called first; the nanny shall be called if the parents cannot be reached. The contact parent will notify the other parent as soon as possible.

3. Religious Instruction

i. The parents will educate and expose the children to religious instruction in keeping with the tradition in place prior to their separation and consistent with the children's best interests.

4. Extracurricular Events and Activities

i. Each parent may enrol the children and/or participate in the activities he or she chooses, provided the activities do not overlap with the other parent's time with the children. The parents shall consult and come to a mutual decision regarding extracurricular activities that overlap both parent's time with the children. Neither parent shall enrol the child in activities that overlap with the other parent's time without that parent's consent.

ii. The parents shall obtain schedules and other necessary information directly from the instructor and/or coaches of the activities. The schedules given to one parent will be photocopied and provided to the other parent.

iii. The parents may attend special events at school and extracurricular activities, such as games, concerts, recitals, shows, or performances. Extended family members are also welcome to attend extracurricular activities.

iv. Birthday parties for the children: the organization of the children's birthday parties will rotate between the parents for each child. For instance, if Joan organized Brenda's 7th birthday then Tom would organize Brenda's 8th birthday. Tom organized David's 9th birthday so Joan will organize David's 10th birthday. Input from the children with respect to their desired activities will be considered. Assistance from the other parent is allowed and encouraged.

5. **The Children's Time with Their Parents**

One of the guiding principles will be that it is preferable for the children to spend time with a parent if he or she is available, rather than the caregiver.

Secondly, the parents are expected to follow these guidelines unless there has been a mutually agreed upon change to the schedule approved by Dr. Irving. No parent shall threaten to withhold the children from the other parent.

a. **Routine or Daily Time-Sharing Schedule**

The children shall reside with both their parents in accordance with the following schedule:

Week ONE

   i. The children shall spend Wednesday from after school until Thursday morning with Tom. Tom will pick up the children at their school and drop them off at school on Thursday morning.

  ii. The children shall also spend the weekend with Tom from Friday after school until Monday morning. Tom will pick up the children at their school on Friday and drop them off at school on Monday morning.

Week TWO

   i. The children shall spend Wednesday from after school until Thursday morning with Tom. Tom will pick up the children at their school and drop them off at school on Thursday morning.

      At all other times, the children will stay with Joan.

b. **Holiday and Special Days Time-Sharing Schedule**
[This can be customized to suit any religious orientation]
The children shall share equal holiday time with their parents in accordance with the following schedule:

School Breaks: The children shall be with Tom for Winter Break on odd-numbered years. On even-numbered years, the children shall be with Joan for Winter Break. This will alternate on a yearly basis.

Easter Weekend: The children shall spend the Easter long weekend with Tom on even-numbered years, and with Joan on odd-numbered years. This will alternate on a yearly basis.

Mother's Day and Father's Day: Joan has the option of having the children from 11:00 a.m. and overnight on Mother's Day regardless of whether it is a scheduled weekend with Tom. Tom has the option of having the children from 11:00 a.m. and overnight on Father's Day regardless of whether it is a scheduled weekend with Joan.

Summer Vacations: The children will spend one uninterrupted week with each parent in July and one uninterrupted week with each parent in August. On odd-numbered years, Tom will notify Joan by March 1 as to which weeks he will be with the children, and she will then notify Tom by April 1 as to which weeks she will be with the children for that year. On even-numbered years, Joan will have the first choice as to which weeks she will be with the children, and she will notify Tom by March 1 of that year. Then Tom will notify Joan by April 1st as to which weeks he will be with the children. The remainder of the children's summer vacation time will revert to the regular/daily schedule.

Thanksgiving: Tom will have the children in 2009 and Joan will have the children in 2010. This will alternate on a yearly basis.

Halloween: Joan will have the children in 2009 and Tom will have the children in 2010. This will alternate on a yearly basis. The parent with whom the children spend Halloween will be responsible for their costumes.

211

Christmas School Break: The Christmas break begins on the last day of school and ends the first morning school resumes. The time period will be shared equally.

On odd-numbered years, the children will spend the first week of the Christmas holidays with Joan and the second week with Tom. On odd-numbered years the children will spend Christmas Eve night and Christmas morning with Joan. On odd-numbered years the children will spend from 2:00 pm Christmas Day until 12:00 pm the following day with Tom.

On even-numbered years, the children will spend the first week of the Christmas holidays with Tom and the second week with Joan. On even-numbered years the children will spend Christmas Eve night and Christmas morning with Tom. On even-numbered years the children will spend from 2:00 p.m. Christmas Day until 12:00 p.m. Boxing Day with Joan.

Children's Birthdays: The children's birthday will revert to the regular/daily schedule or on consent can make other arrangements.

Parents' Birthdays: The children's birthday will revert to the regular/daily schedule or on consent can make other arrangements.

Statutory Holidays: If the Monday immediately following the weekend that the children are with either parent is a statutory holiday, then that parent will keep the children until 7:00 pm on Monday. If the Friday preceding the children's weekend with either parent is a statutory holiday, then that parent's weekend with the children will commence after school on the Thursday.

School Professional Development (PD) Days: If the Monday immediately following the weekend that the children are with either parent is a PD day, then that parent will keep the children until 7:00 p.m. on Monday. If the Friday preceding the children's weekend with either parent is a PD day holiday, then that parent's weekend with the children will commence after school on the Thursday.

c. **Travel**

When one parent is travelling with the children for more than two days and/or 100 [kilometres] away from either home, he or she will provide the other with a complete itinerary, an address and telephone number where he or she can be reached in the event of an emergency. If plane travel is involved then the travelling parent will provide the complete details of flights being taken two weeks in advance of travel.

When possible, the children will speak to the other parent during their holiday period. When travelling a long distance away or with time zones involved it is preferable to arrange in advance when the phone calls will be scheduled. The parents will sign whatever travel authorization forms are needed to support any travel he or she plans to do with the children.

Since the travel authorization forms need to be notarized, the travelling parent will provide the itinerary to the non-travelling parent at least two weeks in advance and the non-travelling parent will prepare the document and have it notarized in time to return it to the travelling parent at least one week prior to departure.

When travel authorization forms or children are not flying, one-week notice for planned travel is suitable.

d. Transitions

  i. Parental Conduct at Transition Points

  (a) At transition points, both parents will behave in accordance with the Parental Guidelines (see section A on pages 3 to 5 of this document).

  ii. Parenting Continuity
  It will be in the best interest of the children if both parents are aware of the events and experiences in the children's lives, including those that occur when the children are with the other parent.

  (a) At transition points and/or at another time mutually preferred, the resident parent will provide the other parent with a brief synopsis of the children's experience.

e. Children's Clothing and Belongings

  i. It is preferable for both parents to have adequate clothing for the children. The clothes the children have worn en route to the time with the other parent will be returned (washed or not) and placed in the children's knapsacks when they return to the other parent.
  ii. The children's belongings belong to them. The children will have the option of taking toys, computer games, and so on back and forth as they wish. As each of them becomes old enough, they will be encouraged to assume responsibility for these items by remembering to bring and return them as they desire.

iii. Major sporting items, dress clothes, and other expensive items will travel back and forth with the children as they desire and/or on the verbal requests of the other parent. The items will be promptly returned with the children. If the item is damaged or broken, the parent who had it when the damage occurred is responsible for replacing the item.

iv. Depending on their age, the children may also be expected to assume some responsibility as determined by the resident parent at the time.

6. Communication

a. Parental Communication

i. The parents shall exert their best efforts to communicate co-operatively with each other. The parents shall communicate via email or telephone about the children's experiences.

ii. The parents shall follow the guideline set out in Appendix A: Parental Communication and Behaviour.

b. Parent-Child Communication

i. The children may call the non-resident parent on the telephone whenever they wish.

ii. The non-resident parent may call the children on the telephone between 7:00pm and 8:00pm. If the children are not available to receive the call and a message is left, the resident parent shall assist the children in returning the call to the other parent.

iii. Both parents shall encourage the children to feel comfortable calling the other parent and shall afford the children the privacy to do so.

c. **Parental Communication with the Children Present**
As part of their normal development, children identify with both their parents. When one parent says negative things about the other parent within earshot of the children, he or she undermines that part of the children that identify with that parent and thus undermines the children's identity and self-esteem.

i. Within earshot of the children, both parents shall conduct themselves in accordance with the Parental Guidelines (see section A on pages 3 to 5 of this document). In particular, they will be supportive of the children's relationship with the other parent and will scrupulously avoid overt conflict between them.

7. **Safety Issues**
The basic rule is "Safety is Number One."

i. Both parents' homes will be childproofed, with extreme caution taken into consideration for electrical outlets, porches, toilets, stairs, and kitchen and bathroom drawers.
ii. The children will only be permitted to travel in a vehicle with properly installed baby/child seats and/or booster seats.
iii. Both parents agree to abide by all safety rules and regulations governing child booster seats.
iv. The best defence against accidents is still supervision. The parents agree that there is no substitution for their eyes and ears.

8. **Unexpected Events**

   Unexpected events are a normal part of everyday life. Traffic, inclement weather, traffic accidents, road closures, and sudden illness are to be expected but not predicted. Consequently, there will be occasions when such events interfere with routine and/or holiday time-sharing schedules.

   a. **Changing the Time-Sharing Schedule**

      i. Should the need arise, the parents will communicate verbally and/or in writing as to a request(s) for a change to the usual or holiday schedule. They will do so with as much notice as possible. A verbal or written response will be provided with 48 hours.

      ii. Each parent will discuss changes to the schedule, first with the other parent and prior to mentioning anything to the children about a change and/or a special activity.

      iii. If additional time is required due to a special event or celebration, notice will be provided to the other parent when the need arises and/or 2 weeks in advance. A response will be provided within 24 hours.

      iv. As a rule, the parents will not be entitled to make up time if they request a change. Notwithstanding the rule, makeup time may be offered.

      v. If, for any reason, one parent cannot be available to care for the children for an overnight period (24 hours) during their scheduled times, the other parent will be given the "first right of refusal" to care for the children. If the other parent cannot accommodate the request, the resident parent is responsible for arranging alternate child care.

    vi. It is understood that traffic and increment weather may cause delays. Notwithstanding, every effort (including allowing for more time if necessary) will be made by the parents to be punctual in their delivery of the children to the other parent, to daycare, to nursery school, or to activities. If one parent cannot deliver the children within 15 minutes of the scheduled time, he or she will notify the other parent when the need for delay arises.

9. Moving Households (Mobility)

a. Moving

    i. Two months' written notice will be provided to the other parent if a residential move is being considered.

    ii. Either parent may move freely within 20 miles of his or her current residence without the consent of the other parent.

    iii. For moves further than 20 miles, the parents will consult with one another as to any changes required to their time-sharing schedules. Neither parent may move without the express written consent of the other parent.

10. Annual Review

No parenting plan is permanent, and all plans require revision over time as the parents' and the children's needs change. Any aspect of the parenting plan may be revised by the parents on mutual consent. Accordingly, the parents will monitor the terms of the parenting plan in relation to the children's ongoing adjustment and will review their plan at least on an annual basis.

11. Dispute Resolution Mechanism

a. Breaking Impasses

    i. When either parent has an issue he or she wishes to resolve with the other parent, he or she will indicate this to the other parent via email, telephone or in person.

   ii. The parents agree that within 7 days of being informed of a problematic issue, or as soon thereafter as is reasonable and practical, they will discuss the issue to see if they can resolve the conflict between themselves. The parents have every confidence they will be able to do so.

  iii. If Tom and Joan are unable to resolve a parenting issue, they will attend mediation in an attempt to resolve the issue with Howard Irving. If Dr. Irving is unwilling or unable to act, then the parties will agree on his replacement.

Howard H. Irving, Ph.D., AccFM (FMC)
Toronto, ON

Dated _____the city of _____.

_____
Joan

_____
Witness to the signature of Joan Smith

Dated _____ the city of _____.

_____
Tom

_____
Witness to the signature of Tom Smith

Notes

1. D.B. King, "Accentuate the Positive — Eliminate the Negative," *Family and Conciliation Courts Review* 31, no. 1 (1993): 9–28.
2. Howard H. Irving and Michael Benjamin, *Therapeutic Family Mediation* (Thousand Oaks, CA: Sage Publications Inc., 2002): 340–73.
3. W.J. Everett, "Shared Parenting in Divorce," *Journal of Law and Religion* 2, no. 1 (1984): 85–99.
4. Hugh McIsaac, from Preface in *Family Mediation Contemporary Issues*, by Howard H. Irving and Michael Benjamin (Thousand Oaks, CA: Sage Publications, 1995), IX–X.
5. From the booklet, *Stress and the Divorced*, published by Hoffmann-LaRoche Limited, Vaudreuil, Quebec, 1972–73.
6. *National Post*, January 13, 2008.
7. Harvey Brownstone, quoted in *Tug of War: A Judge's Verdict on Separation, Custody Battles, and the Bitter Realities of Family Court* (Toronto: ECW Press, 2009); foreword by Paula J. Hepner, XVI–XVII.
8. M. Patrician, "'Twas the Night Before Court," *Conciliation Court Review* 21, no. 1: 95–96.
9. Paula J. Hepner, *Tug of War*, XVI–XVII.
10. Mel Roman and William F. Haddad, *The Disposable Parent* (New York: Holt, Rinehart and Winston, 1978): 54.

11. Belinda Rachman, "How to Divorce Without Killing Each Other in the Process," accessed October 12, 2010, at *searchwarp.com/swa260181.htm.*
12. Robert Weiss, quoted by O.J. Coogler, in "Changing the Lawyer's Role in Matrimonial Practice," *Conciliation Courts Review* 15 (September 1977): 3.
13. Herbert Glieberman, quoted by O.J. Coogler, in "Changing the Lawyer's Role in Matrimonial Practice," *Conciliation Courts Review* 15 (September 1977): 2–3.
14. Alberta Teachers' Association pamphlet.
15. Family Court of Milwaukee, Bill of Rights of Children in Divorce Actions.
16. Pamphlet: *Parents Are Forever*, Association of Family and Conciliation Courts.
17. National Committee on Violence against Women.
18. *The Autocrat of the Breakfast-Table* (1858). A collection of essays by Oliver Wendell Holmes, Sr.
19. Howard H. Irving and Michael Benjamin, *Therapeutic Family Mediation* (Thousand Oaks, CA: Sage Publications, 2002).
20. Howard H. Irving, et al., "A Comparative Analysis of Two Family Court Services: An Exploratory Study of Conciliation Counselling" (Ministry of the Attorney General of Ontario, 1979): 561–69.
21. Isolina Ricci, *Mom's House, Dad's House: Making Two Homes for Your Child*, 2nd edition (New York: Simon & Shuster, 1997).
22. Ibid., 7, 11, 17.
23. Isolina Ricci, *Mom's House, Dad's House: Making Two Homes for Your Child*, 2nd edition (New York: Simon & Shuster, 1997).
24 Howard H. Irving and Michael Benjamin, *Therapeutic Family Mediation: Helping Families Resolve Conflict* (Thousand Oak, CA: Sage, 2000): 340–73.
25. Isolina Ricci, *Mom's House, Dad's House: Making Two*

Home for Your Child, 2nd edition (New York: Simon & Shuster, 1997): 51, 83, 89–92.

26. Ibid., 91, 95, 104, 108.
27. Ibid., 90, 95, 117.
28. Ibid., 125, 130, 142–153.
29. Frederick G. Gans, "The Non-Custodial Parent. A Personal View," a monograph published by the Department of Continuing Education, The Law Society of Upper Canada, Osgoode Hall, Toronto.
30. Judith S. Wallerstein and Julia Lewis, "The Long-Term Impact of Divorce on Children," *Family and Conciliation Courts Review* 36, no. 3 (1998): 368–82.
31. D.T. Saposnek, "Working with Children in Mediation," (Ch. 8, 156, 164–65) in *Divorce and Family Mediation*, edited by Jay Folberg (New York: Ann Milne & Peter Salem Guilford Press, 2004).
32. Pamphlet, *Parents Are Forever*, Association of Family and Conciliation Courts.
33. Valerie J. Botter, "Divorce, Kids and Dating: Creative Solutions for Family Transitions," December 2005, accessed at *www.botterlaw.com/DivorceKidsDating.htm*, October 12, 2010.
34. *National Post*, September 22, 2010.

Sources

PUBLICATIONS

Ahrons, Constance. *A Good Divorce: Keeping Your Family Together When Your Marriage Comes Apart.* New York: HarperCollins Publishers, 1995.

Ahrons, Constance. *We're Still Family: What Grown Children Have to Say About Their Parents' Divorce.* New York: HarperCollins Publishers, 2005.

Brownstone, Harvey. *Tug of War: A Judge's Verdict on Separation, Custody Battles, and the Bitter Realities of Family Court.* Toronto: ECW Press, 2009.

Bush, Robert A. Baruch, and Joseph P. Folger. *The Promise of Mediation: Responding to Conflict Through Empowerment and Recognition.* San Francisco: Jossey-Bass, 1994.

Coogler, O.J. *Structured Mediation in Divorce Settlement: A Handbook for Marital Mediators.* Lanham, MD: Lexington Books, 1978.

Dreman, S. "The Influence of Divorce on Children." *Journal of Divorce and Remarriage* 32 (2000): 3–4.

Emery, Robert E. *The Truth About Children and Divorce: Dealing with the Emotions So You and Your Children Can Thrive.* New York; Plume, 2006.

Fellman, Gordon. *Rambo and the Dalai Lama.* Albany, NY: Suny Press, 1991.

Fisher, Robert, William Ury, and Bruce Patton. *Getting to Yes: Negotiating Agreement Without Giving In.* New York: Penguin, 1983.

Folberg, Jay, Ann L. Milne, and Peter Salem. *Divorce and Family Mediation: Models, Techniques, and Applications.* New York: Guilford Press, 2004.

Girdner, L.K. "Mediation Triage: Screening for Spouse Abuse in Divorce Mediation." *Mediation Quarterly* 7 (1990): 4.

Irving, Howard H. *Divorce Mediation.* Toronto: Personal Library Publishing Inc., 1980. United States: Universe Press, 1981.

———. *Family Mediation. Theory and Practice with Chinese Families.* Hong Kong: University Press, 2002.

Irving, Howard H., and Michael Benjamin. *Therapeutic Family Mediation.* Thousand Oaks, CA: Sage Publications, 2002.

———. *Family Mediation: Contemporary Issues.* Thousand Oaks, CA: Sage Publications, 1995.

———. "Research in Family Mediation: Review and Implications," *Mediation Quarterly* 13, no. 1 (Autumn 1995): 53–82.

Irving, Howard H., Michael Benjamin, and N. Trocme. "Shared Parenting: An Empirical Analysis Utilizing a Large Data Base." *Family Process* 23 (December 1984): 561–69.

Kelly, Joan B. "Current Research on Children's Postdivorce Adjustment — No Simple Answers." *Family and Conciliation Courts Review* 31, no. 1 (January 1993): 29–49.

Ricci, Isolina. *Mom's House, Dad's House: Making Two Homes for Your Child* (2nd edition) New York: Simon & Shuster, 1997.

Saposnek, Donald T. *Mediating Child Custody Disputes: A Strategic Approach* (revised edition). San Francisco: Jossey-Bass, 1998.

Wallerstein, Judith S., and Joan B. Kelly. *Surviving the Breakup: How Children and Parents Cope with Divorce.* New York: Basic Books, 1980.

Warshak, Richard. "Blanket Restrictions: Overnight Contact Between Parents and Young Children." *Family and Conciliation Courts Review* 38, no. 4 (October 2000): 422–45.

———. *Divorce Poison: Protecting the Parent–Child Bond From A Vindictive Ex.* New York: Regan Books, 2003.

WEBSITES

Association for Conflict Resolution
www.acresolution.org/index.html

Association of Family and Conciliation Courts
www.afccnet.org

Divorceinfo
www.divorceinfo.com

Everything Mediation
www.mediate.com

Family Mediation Canada
www.fmc.ca

Family Mediation in Canada: Implications for women's equality
www.swc-cfc.gc.ca/index-eng.html

Howard H. Irving (personal website)
www.howardirving.com

Mediators information
www.mediators.org

Society of Professionals in Dispute Resolution
www.spidr.org

Index